UK Web Women

The internet guide for work and play

by

Louise Proddow

Orders: Please contact Bookpoint Ltd, 78 Milton Park,
Abingdon, Oxon OX14 4TD. Telephone: (44) 01235 827720,
Fax: (44) 01235 400454. Lines are open from 9.00 – 6.00, Monday
to Saturday, with a 24 hour message answering service.
Email address: orders@bookpoint.co.uk

British Library Cataloguing in Publication Data
A catalogue record for this title is available from The British Library

ISBN 0 340 80414 9

First published 2001
Impression number   10 9 8 7 6 5 4 3 2 1
Year   2007 2006 2005 2004 2003 2002 2001

Typeset and Design by

Printed in Spain for Hodder & Stoughton Educational,
a division of Hodder Headline Plc, 338 Euston Road,
London NW1 3BH by **Graphycems**.

I want to dedicate this book to.....My Mum

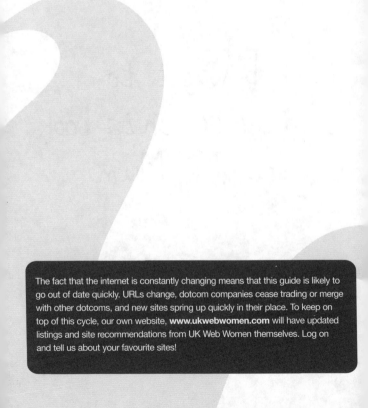

The fact that the internet is constantly changing means that this guide is likely to go out of date quickly. URLs change, dotcom companies cease trading or merge with other dotcoms, and new sites spring up quickly in their place. To keep on top of this cycle, our own website, **www.ukwebwomen.com** will have updated listings and site recommendations from UK Web Women themselves. Log on and tell us about your favourite sites!

Acknowledgment

The ever-changing internet is inspirational and opening up new opportunities for everyone. A big thanks to all the people who share my passionate belief in the net, especially Richard Perry and Sara Adamson whose enthusiasm and support helped shape the book and bring it to life, together with the backing of Gary Brine and Graham Dodridge at Gyro.

Special thanks to Rachel Sharman who brought the words to life with her wonderful illustrations, and to Gyro's design team of Victoria DelaRoch, Christopher Smith, Robert Wilson, Michelle Henley and Charlie Loft. To Nicola Beck who cheerfully assisted, as did Sarah Walker, Fiona Butler and Mike Abbott. To Carl Geraghty at NOP, who helped with the research. Also to www.handbag.com for hosting the www.ukwebwomen.com website.

Thanks to David and Alex for giving me the freedom to write and research when I should have been spending time with them. Thanks also to the team at Sun Microsystems for their insightful vision, which actively empowers employees and customers.

And finally, thanks to Tim Gregson-Williams at Hodder & Stoughton, and all those women who have shared their stories with me for this book. I hope that UK Web Women, and your internet journey, makes you smile, and brings you fun, excitement and new, positive life experiences.

Contents

Introduction

The internet is everywhere. More users are going online daily, especially women. It's transforming our lives. Entrepreneurs, teenagers, women of all ages and backgrounds are getting online to a world of possibilities, networking, homeworking and getting answers to questions on every conceivable subject. There was a time when you could get by and not be connected, but today it's an integral part of communication, of how we work, how we play, how we run our lives. No–one can afford to ignore what the net has to offer.

This guide is about sharing with you the online experiences of women across the UK. Showing you the many ways you can use the internet to enhance your relationships, career, health and wealth. As you surf through the book you will discover the diverse range of roles the net can play in your life, helping with everything from bringing up a family to starting a business, from getting a mortgage to keeping in touch with friends.

Discovering the true potential of the net is about so much more than just logging on. It's about using the net to run your life differently. It's about changing pre–conceived ideas and moving beyond traditional ways of doing things. This may sound a bold claim when most internet books focus on listing websites. Yes, knowing which are the best sites to visit is important, but the net also goes beyond this. It's about starting to think in new ways, using the online resources to change the way you do things. This guide will help you get started on your journey through the possibilities of the internet.

The net is a great equaliser in our personal and professional lives. It's an information and community resource which can be used to remove many of the barriers that have held us back in the past. Section by section you'll discover how to use the net to leap ahead. Online learning has become more accessible, online discussion groups provide a great way to develop confidence in new areas and explore ideas. Networking with others around the world, or doing your own research – the net allows women to hook up to new perspectives and fresh attitudes.

What's more, the research detailed throughout the guide will show you this is not just optimistic talk – it's fact that the internet empowers women. The facts speak for themselves; our case studies show how women across the UK are all benefiting from getting online. It's exciting that this is only early days in women's online adventures as the net itself develops and expands at an astonishing rate, and as more women are taking the plunge and getting online.

Whether you are already a confident surfer or simply thinking about getting online, I hope this guide will benefit you, and help you uncover a world of possibilities. Getting online is not complicated, all you need to do is grasp the basics and you'll be on your way! Throughout the book you will find some helpful hints and tips to help get you started, as well as listing over a thousand of the top websites to help you find your way around the net.

Use this guide to fuel your imagination – log on to our website, **www.ukwebwomen.com**, to get the latest updates, a place to network with other UK web women, find updates to this book, and share your internet stories. **www.ukwebwomen.com** is produced in association with **www.handbag.com**. Let's embrace the net together and get logged on to an exciting future.

Chapter 1

Women Online

More UK women than ever before are embracing the net and logging on to the exciting mix of content, services and resources on offer. Getting online is easier and cheaper than it has ever been. With barriers to easy internet access a thing of the past, the net opens up new opportunities for women. Whether you want to be studious, smart, humourous, supportive, a little crazy or practical, the net has more than enough to keep you occupied.

The number of women online is growing at an amazing rate with almost 8 million UK women logging on in the last twelve months – we make up 42% of the UK online population, and the gap is closing fast. The internet increasingly plays a central role in all aspects of our lives. It's a new club, a great place to come together, to meet and have fun.

Women's modern lives are busy; our careers, businesses and families mean we have to juggle our commitments to balance work and home life. The internet is the modern day saviour to help our hectic schedules. No wonder so many women are finding sites that can save them time, money and energy. It empowers women by offering a unique opportunity to network with other women, to work from home, shop online and do a whole host of other exciting and time-saving activities. Not to mention instant communication and networking.

Personal communication leads the way as the most popular online activity, followed by sites that give information and services on holidays, education, home shopping and leisure and travel. Your life can benefit from the tremendous amount of resources on the internet. Whether you are a working mother trying to find more time in your hectic schedule, or a mature woman looking for more challenges and new interests, the net should be your first point of call.

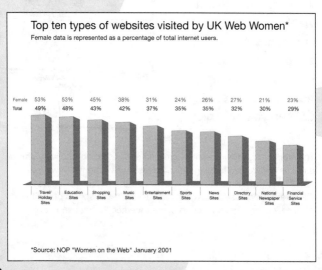

Top ten types of websites visited by UK Web Women*
Female data is represented as a percentage of total internet users.

	Travel/ Holiday Sites	Education Sites	Shopping Sites	Music Sites	Entertainment Sites	Sports Sites	News Sites	Directory Sites	National Newspaper Sites	Financial Service Sites
Female	53%	53%	45%	38%	31%	24%	26%	27%	21%	23%
Total	49%	48%	43%	42%	37%	35%	35%	32%	30%	29%

*Source: NOP "Women on the Web" January 2001

Top 12 issues women say matter to them:*

1   Balancing paid work and home life

2   Support for looking after children and caring duties

3   The pay gap between men and women and maximising women's potential at work

4   Getting women's voices heard

5   Teenage issues like education and career choices, positive role models, mixed social messages and teenage pregnancies

6   Violence against women

7   Health issues

8   Female–friendly financial advice

9   Support for women setting up in business

10 Recognising the diversity of women

11 Recognition of all the roles women play

12 How Government can communicate more effectively with women

*Source: Cabinet Office Womens Unit

The internet can help address the issues that matter to women the most, by providing information and support in those areas.

Women and girls of all ages are spending more time online discovering new activities. From teenage entertainment sites to educational research to planning a family to getting financial advice – the internet is becoming an integral part of our everyday lives. At work, rest and play lives are changing, as our real life stories from women of all ages from across the UK reveal.

Case Study
Sally Mabey

"I'm the current Press Officer for the Glamorgan Federation of Women's Institutes. When I was appointed, I realised our Federation wasn't making the most of the internet. It provides the ideal medium for us to communicate with our members and provide information to the general public, as well as link into the Women's Institute network and its affiliates all over the world. The net is definitely the path of the future, and I liked the idea of getting on board sooner rather than later. The Women's Institute has already developed a strong online presence, at **www.womens–institute.org.uk.**

"We were the second Federation to go online, launching at the end of October last year. It took me a long time to persuade our more sceptical members of the benefits of the internet, since they were worried about the potential expense, but now we are up and running, we haven't looked back! Now lots more Federations have websites, as they have seen how well it has been working for us."

"On our site, at **www.glamorganfwi.org.uk**, surfers can find out information on our activities, events, latest news and even get information on joining the WI. I built the website myself, with a little help from my husband and daughter. I had no experience of web design before, but managed to work it out, using a simple website programme called Adobe PageMaker (which was sometimes a little too simple!) and have recently started learning html, which is the programming language used for the internet."

"At home, I use the net for absolutely everything it can be used for: looking up train times and booking tickets on **www.thetrainline.com**, and puzzles and quizzes which I do with my husband. My favourite site is **www.worldwidewords.org**, which is all about words and the English language. The web is such a great resource, it's like an infinite library, only without labels, so finding your way around can be tricky!"

What is the internet?

The internet is simply just one very large computer network. Estimates vary, but the general consensus is that there are currently around 100,000 computer networks connected together, supporting some 350 million users worldwide. In the UK alone, over 13 million people access the internet every day.

Some of these computers are connected together on local area networks installed in corporations. Others connect to the network from people's homes via modems and telephone lines. But however the connection is made, all the computers share a common language, which allows them to interact and work together.

Because all the computers on the internet share a common networking language, it doesn't matter what make of computer they are, nor what operating system they're running. This means that you can plug almost any type of computer into the network and it will then be able to talk directly to any of the other connected computers.

Anyone with the right equipment can connect to the net and become part of it. All you need is an internet device – which could be a computer with modem (either a PC or an Apple Mac) and phone line, a mobile phone or a TV and set-top box. Many newer computer systems come internet–ready. You can find out more about connecting to the net in the next chapter.

Feminising the net

At last the net has come of age, attracting a diversity of users as well as content. Geeky men in anoraks no longer dominate the web. In the US the number of women using the internet exceeded the number of men for the first time in summer 2000, a trend which is already evident in the UK and around the world. As Jupiter MMXI figures highlight, more women are going online as the internet develops.

Web facts – Women on the web

- Over the last year 18.9 million people aged over 15 used the internet in the UK

- The number of UK women online is growing fast, with 7.95 million female users in December 2000, an increase of over two million in twelve months

- The online gender gap is closing. The rate women are going online is growing at a faster rate than men, with women making up 42% of surfers now, compared with 40% a year ago

- The average UK female surfer uses the internet 7.31 times a week, for an average of 54 minutes per visit

- When using the web female surfers are very loyal, with 31% visiting 1–2 sites, 39% 3–5, 11% 6–9, 10% 10–19 and 6% visiting more than twenty websites regularly

- Women visit sites that are practical and help them save time and money, like those that focus on shopping, travel, careers and finance

- The most popular use of the internet with 78% is personal communication, compared with home shopping at 33%

- The most frequently-purchased goods on the net are books and music

Source: NOP "Women on the Web" January 2001

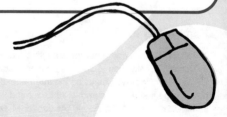

Getting online can help women make the most of their hectic schedules. You can order your weekly shopping from your computer, and get it delivered to your home. You can work from home, connecting to the office on a computer network, using e-mail to keep in touch.

The internet has also made flexible working options more widely available. These new working patterns have become much more important to working mothers in particular, who need to balance their work life with raising their children. In 1999, nearly a quarter of women had flexible working arrangements compared to around 15% of men. Once they are online at home, they can keep in touch with the office quickly and easily – logging on whenever is convenient to keep up to date with their e-mails and on top of the work situation.

With around 25% of all new businesses being run by women, the internet also enables even more women to branch out on their own and work flexibly from home, in easy contact with customers, suppliers and work colleagues, online.

Communications on the net

Research has shown that the primary use of the internet by women is for communication – using e-mail to keep in touch with work as well as family and friends all over the world. The power of e-mail means you can send letters instantly and cheaply to anywhere, world-wide. The world has become a smaller and friendlier place, now that chatrooms and online communities have brought diverse groups of people together, creating new kinds of friendships and interactions. Women are benefiting from the support offered by online networking groups, and from the ease of contact with friends and family, no matter where they are located. The internet enables women to focus on what they do best – communication.

Case Study
Zelda Tolley

"Up until January 1999 I was working full-time, juggling career and family as we women do. I use the net for everything from e-mailing friends and family to shopping for groceries and paying my bills. My favourite search engine, **www.google.com**, helps me find new sites every day!

"My world changed when I was diagnosed with breast cancer. I'm now through the treatment and hopefully recovered, but life is no longer the same. I emerged from the chemotherapy with little hair, no job but a fledgling greetings card business, which I took online. My first web site **www.zjtcards.co.uk** was a joint effort with my son and a showcase for my cards. My latest venture and all my own work is **www.puertopollensa.com**, devoted to our favourite holiday resort of Puerto Pollensa in Mallorca. Now I am no longer just a passive consumer of the web but an active participant. The beauty of running a website is that it can be managed anytime, from anywhere. Talk about flexible working! I have no ambitions to be the next dot com millionaire. But I do hope to produce a reasonable income and to have fun doing it."

Women's sites

With the demise of the online gender gap, women are attracting a lot of attention. Big brands and big budgets are being invested to meet the needs of women of all ages online. Websites are fighting to win the web loyalty of women.

The enthusiastic explosion of women online has sparked the growth of female-focused sites. They offer advice and information on subjects that matter to women, from childcare to relationships, celebrity gossip to networking. The immediate appeal of these women's portals is obvious: they understand women and deliver great content.

The early US pioneer **www.women.com** attracts a lot of visitors from the UK and **www.ivillage.com** has now moved to our shores in a joint partnership with Tesco to launch **www.ivillage.co.uk**. One of our home grown portals, **www.handbag.com**, has already climbed into the top slot in many league tables, offering a broad range of content from shopping to childcare, to managing your busy life. Women's sites are a great place to gather information, make contact with other women, or go shopping.

The choice the internet offers is amazing, with advice, fashions, new friendships, and some great bargains. Some of this may sound a little superficial but the truth is the internet also has a powerful role to play in redressing the gender balance, by opening up communication, resources and opportunities to women. Whether you want to start a new business or create a new network of contacts the internet can help. It gives new practical choices and information that truly empowers us all. The net can have a life changing impact, creating the chance to work from home, to find new ways to manage your time and giving you the motivation to get healthier. So get online and join millions of other women as they explore the possibilities created by the internet!

You know it's time to log on when:

- You want to empower yourself
- You want to network and meet people with similar interests
- You want to keep in touch with distant friends and relatives
- You want to be part of the information age
- You feel like some retail therapy in the middle of the night

Distribution of the 7.95 million UK Women on the web*

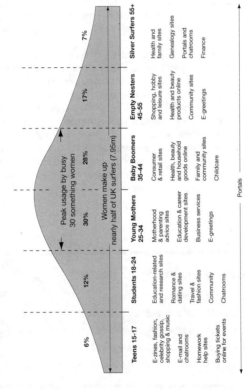

	Teens 15-17	Students 18-24	Young Mothers 25-34	Baby Boomers 35-44	Empty Nesters 45-55	Silver Surfers 55+
%	6%	12%	30%	28%	17%	7%
	E-zines, fashion, celebrity gossip, shopping & music	Education-related and research sites	Motherhood & parenting advice sites	Consumer & retail sites	Shopping, hobby and leisure sites	Health and family sites
	E-mail and chatrooms	Romance & dating sites	Education & career development sites	Health, beauty and household goods online	Health and beauty products online	Genealogy sites
	Homework help sites	Travel & fashion sites	Business services	Family and community sites	Community sites	Portals and chatrooms
	Buying tickets online for events	Community	E-greetings	Childcare	E-greetings	Finance
		Chatrooms				

Peak usage by busy 30 something women

Women make up nearly half of UK surfers (7.95m)

Portals

"Women are attracted to sites that offer practical, everyday services relevant to their lifestage"

*Based on statistics from NOP

Chapter 2

Getting Online

If you're nervous about the complexities of the internet, don't be! There's a new internet user every second, and if they can do it, so can you! It's not just for techie men, either: women aged 25-40 make up over 60% of new internet users.

How to get connected

Basically, all you need to get started is a computer, a modem, a phone line and an account with an Internet Service Provider (ISP). You can even connect to the net without using a computer, using a smaller, more mobile device, like a mobile phone, instead!

1) Getting the hardware

Hardware is a term which refers to the physical parts of your computer, like the screen, the hard drive, the keyboard and mouse. There are basic features you will need in order to be able to access the internet with a computer. These are: hard drive size of at least 500-megabytes, 8-megabytes of RAM (memory), a Pentium processor, an operating system like Windows 2000, and, if you want to be able to get sound from the net, a sound card and speakers. If these specifications are all a foreign language to you, don't worry! There's lots of help available online and from other sources like magazines if you're buying a computer, and the basic features are pretty standard to all new computers. The latest computers are not only surprisingly inexpensive but often already have everything you need to connect to the internet, such as a modem and internet software. Often it's just a case of plugging in, switching on and the computer will automatically dial up the internet to set up a connection!

Buying a computer

You can buy a computer on the high street, over the phone and even on the internet. Some of the biggest suppliers are:

High street:

Dixons at **www.dixons.co.uk**
Tempo at **www.tempo.co.uk**
Currys at **www.currys.co.uk**
PC World at **www.pcworld.co.uk**
Comet at **www.comet.co.uk**

Own-label:

Time at **www.timegroup.co.uk**
IBM at **www.ibm.com**
Gateway at **www.gateway.com**
Viglen at **www.viglen.co.uk**
Compaq at **www.compaq.co.uk**
Dell at **www.dell.co.uk**

Best value deals:

www.jungle.com
www.letsbuyit.com
www.unbeatable.co.uk.

2) Modem and phone line

A modem is the device that connects your
computer to the internet, via a phone line.
You probably will already have a modem inside
your computer, if not you'll have to get a separate
one to get online. The modem is what enables you
to download information from the internet to your
computer, so the faster your modem, the quicker you'll
be able to move around the net, and it will also be faster
for you to access large internet files containing music and films.
For this reason, it's worth getting the fastest modem you can afford –
most modems have a speed of 56kbps (kilobits – bits of information –
per second). You'll soon regret not shelling out when you're stuck on a
slow connection, waiting endlessly for a site to download.

You'll also need a phone line – you can either use your existing line, or
get a second one, just for the net. Using a normal phone line is fine, and
it's probably the easiest way to start gaining web experience. However,
if you're planning on using the web a lot, it might be worth researching
other connection options. Normal phone lines can be slow, because the
capacity of the line is often too small, and this slows down download
times. There are a number of alternatives to using your phone line, such
as digital lines like ISDN and ADSL, which should enable you to greatly
increase the speed of your connection. BT's OpenWorld service, at
www.bt.com/adsl, Telewest's **www.blueyonder.co.uk** and NTL's
www.ntl.com, are all providers of high speed and unmetered internet
access, and are well worth investigating. At the moment, these
technologies are still being developed and installed around the country,
so they may not be available in your area yet – but soon, it will be the
norm to connect to the net in this way. Eventually, it is thought that
everyone will have home access through these high-speed, high
capacity lines, which will be permanently connected to the net
– no need to log on and off!

3) How do I choose an ISP?

Once you have a computer, modem and phone line you need to talk to an Internet Service Provider (ISP) who will connect you to the net. In actual fact, you'll be connecting to the ISP's own big modem. In turn, the big computer (or 'server' as it is called – and Sun Microsystems' servers provide the backbone for most of the internet), will have a permanent connection to the internet.

To get help with your choice of ISP, internet magazines run monthly performance charts with comprehensive listings of the top free and charging ISPs. It may help to ask friends who are already online and get recommendations. See online resources like **www.internet–magazine.com/resource**, and **www.net4nowt.com**. The most important features of a good ISP will be its connection speeds, how reliable it is, how good its customer care is, and how much it charges.

With more than 100 ISPs to choose from in the UK, it's tempting to opt for those which provide the cheapest internet access – but they don't always provide the best service. On the whole, the bigger the company, the better the service. The major ISPs have more modems, more servers and connections capable of transmitting more data, so they're going to be faster, have fewer problems during busy periods and break down less frequently. However, there are now many ISPs who are 'free'. They don't charge a monthly fee, but you may have to pay for technical support and of course, your phone bill.

If you decide to use a free ISP, it is worth noting that they tend to use premium-rate phone lines for their help desks (they have to make their money somewhere!). They may not even have a phone service, and you'll have to pick up the installation CD on the high street, or download the software from the net.

See the list at the end of this chapter for a list of the UK's biggest ISPs.

4) Connecting to the internet and configuring your ISP account

Your account with an ISP will include your own e-mail address and maybe your own web page. Once you have signed up with your chosen ISP, you will need to configure your computer so that it knows how to access the internet. This is less technical than it sounds! Your ISP may provide you with an installation CD, which you simply run, and it automatically sets everything up for you. Or, even easier, configuration details may already be on your computer. Configuring your ISP will automatically install the two most useful programs which you need for working online – a web browser and an e-mail program. A browser is the computer program you use to access the internet. The two most popular programs are Netscape's Navigator and Microsoft's Internet Explorer. There are both quite straightforward to use, and you will probably get one supplied to you with your computer package, if you have decided to buy a new computer. Once you've installed your browser program, you're then all set for the net!

Tip

If you really have trouble getting online, your ISP will usually have a helpline you can call **to talk you through the procedure, and solve any problems you might encounter. Even better, try and persuade a friend with more technological know-how, to come and help!**

Case Study
Jenny Whitehead

"With my family constantly using the internet on our home PC, I felt it was finally time for me to get involved in the online revolution. The only problem is, finding a time when the computer is free so I can practice using the net. I am also not particularly confident on the internet or with computers in general – I always feel I might press the wrong button and delete all the files! I like to surf the net when there's someone from my net-proficient family in the house, just so I can get help if I need it.

"At the moment, I don't get the chance to use the internet every day. I'm so busy, it seems a waste to go online for the sake of it without having a specific goal in mind, and I also worry about the phone bills. However, when I have a reason to go on the internet, I enjoy it, and I'm improving steadily. I have taken some classes in computers which are helping me head in the right direction, even if at the beginning the classes were a bit bewildering! It's good to know that I'm not the only woman still getting the hang of internet surfing – other women I've spoken to have similar difficulties to me. I know it's just a matter of practice, practice, practice until I'm as internet proficient as my husband and daughters."

Connecting to the web without using a computer

It has now become possible to connect to the internet with a variety of new devices, like your mobile phone and your television. It's very early days for these devices, and there may be teething problems. However, the systems are developing incredibly fast, and it has been estimated that within five years time the majority of internet users will not access via a computer, but via one of the following options:

Digital television

Digital television has now become interactive, with systems such as Open and Sky Digital offering services like shopping, banking and e-mail, using your television set as the interface. They are not able to access the full internet as yet, just selected content available on the interactive TV system. Log on to **www.ondigital.co.uk** and **www.skydigital.com** to see the services they provide.

WAP phones and PDAs

Certain mobile phones currently have the ability to log on to the web, and access sites that are WAP (Wireless Application Protocol)-enabled. Some hand-held Personal Digital Assistants are also set to be WAP-enabled. This is predicted to be the main way that people will access the web in the future, with everything you need, from cinema listings to stock prices, available in the palm of your hand.

Try **www.genie.co.uk** or **http://uk.mobile.yahoo.com** to see what the future will look like.

Case Study
Julie Cass

"I started using computers 3 years ago. I had been in a job I didn't enjoy, which was making me unhappy and unconfident. I decided to change jobs and went to work in a residential home, which gave me the opportunity to work with a computer. Although I hadn't really used a computer before, I took to it like a duck to water, and within two weeks of starting my new job had bought my own PC for use at home.

"My son, who is now nearly six, was born with a rare medical condition. My sister, Maxine, had logged on to the internet to get information, and had contacted other sufferers around the world on my behalf. Best of all, she encouraged me to go online myself. She installed Freeserve for me and my internet journey began!

"My prime reason for going online at first was to get information regarding my son's condition. Due to problems associated with this condition, his consultant had advised that we take him off dairy products for a while. I went to **www.stampcollection.co.uk**, the homepage of Terence Stamp's food company, who specialise in making wheat and dairy-free foods, to find out more. I was even able to e-mail the company and received a very kind reply back, with lots of information.

"The internet has also been helpful for my own health. A friend recently told me about the 'death test' on **www.thespark.com**, a quiz that determines how much longer you can expect to live! Although the test is just for fun, it's really opened my eyes to the importance of taking care of yourself and I have set a date to give up smoking in the near future."

If getting online might seem a little daunting at first, and a hassle, it's worth bearing in mind that you only need to do it once! You don't have to be a cybergeek, or even at all technologically proficient to connect to the net. Millions of people all over the world are already benefitting from having the internet in their lives – don't let any technology inhibitions prevent you from joining them!

You know it's time to log on when:

- Everyone's talking about the internet and you don't know what it is
- Your local phone company is providing high-speed access in your area
- You get a fixed-rate service – no more worrying about the phone bill

Sites to help you get online

Advice for getting online

www.theinternetexplained.co.uk is a great starting point if you're new to the web.

www.internet-magazine.com is the online site of the popular internet magazine.

www.net4nowt.com has all the ins and outs of the free ISPs.

www.myhelpdesk.com will give you free internet advice online to solve all your computing problems.

Buying a PC or internet device

www.pcpro.co.uk has the latest reviews on PC's to help you make the right choice. **www.dixons.co.uk** sells computers online, as well as having high street shops. Similar sites include **www.comet.co.uk**, **www.currys.co.uk** and **www.pcworld.co.uk**. **www.unbeatable.co.uk** claims to offer the best prices on the latest technology from all the major brand names. **www.jungle.com** offers great deals on computers and other electrical equipment.

UK Online Initiative

UK Online Centres

The Government has pledged £252 million to ensure everyone will have access to the internet by 2005. UK Online Centres are a new network of learning centres offering access and support for those new to computers and the internet. To find out more about UK Online Centres, call **08080 100 400**, or log on to **www.ukonline.gov.uk**.

Learndirect

Learndirect is an internet service running through the UK Online Centres, offering flexible, high quality learning on a range of subjects, particularly technology. Call **0800 100 900** for more information on learndirect or log on to **www.learndirect.co.uk**.

The BBC has a site designed to help new users become more confident and knowledgeable surfers, at **www.bbc.co.uk/webwise**.

The e-skills National Training Organisation aims to improve the general IT user skills of the workforce and offers modern apprenticeships. Go to **www.e-skillsnto.org.uk** to find out more.

Happy Computers, at **www.happy.co.uk**, aims to make learning about computers fun.

See the *Education Online* chapter for more details on finding computer and internet courses.

UK ISPs

ISPs	Telephone	Website
AOL	0800 376 5432	www.aol.co.uk
BT Internet	0800 800 0001	www.btinternet.com
CIX	020 8255 5050	www.cix.net.uk
ClaraNet		www.clara.net
CompuServe	0990 000 200	www.compuserve.com
Demon Internet	0845 272 2666	www.demon.net
Easynet	020 7681 4444	www.easynet.co.uk
Gemsoft	0114 275 7070	www.gemsoft.net
Genie	09063 020 220	www.genie.co.uk
Global Internet	0870 909 8042	www.global.net.uk
Netcom	0870 566 8008	www.netcom.net.uk
Netscape	0901 900 9000	www.netscapeonline.co.uk
UUNet	0500 474 739	www.uk.uu.net

Free ISPs		
Breathe	09067 112209	www.breathe.com
Freeserve	0870 901 6000	www.freeserve.com
FreeUK	0853 55 55 55	www.freeuk.com
LineOne	0906 308 0100	www.lineone.net
NTL	0800 183 1234	www.ntl.com
Screaming Net	0800 376 5262	www.screaming.net
Tesco.net	0906 3020 111	www.tesco.net
Virgin.net		www.virgin.net
X–stream		www.X–stream.co.uk
Handbag	0906 302 0048	www.handbag.com

Your Guide to E-mail

Electronic mail (or e-mail for short) is the most popular online activity for UK Web Women, and one of the main reasons why people get connected in the first place. In fact, many people subscribe to the internet just for e-mail. It allows you to keep in touch with friends and family all over the world – all you need is their e-mail addresses. It's much quicker than traditional mail – a message can be sent across the world in just a few seconds. And it's much cheaper – it costs the same to send an e-mail to someone in Australia as to your next-door neighbour.

As one teenage Web Woman, Maria James, points out: "Using e-mail I can keep in contact with my boyfriend. He lives in America, and snail mail would take a week to reach him. I also use it to send free text messages to my friends who live locally."

23

E-mail is not just for sending written messages. You can send and receive files, such as photographs, graphics, even video clips, just as quickly and efficiently as messages. Until recently you had to have a computer to send and receive e-mail. But now, an ever-growing range of simple devices, from mobile phones to TVs, have the capability.

Small wonder then, that e-mail is quickly becoming the most common method of communication in the world, overtaking the post, fax and telephone. Over 2 billion e-mails are sent every day!

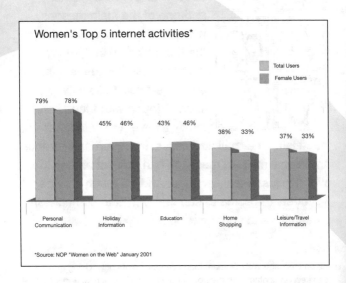

Women's Top 5 internet activities*

Total Users
Female Users

79% 78%
45% 46%
43% 46%
38% 33%
37% 33%

Personal Communication
Holiday Information
Education
Home Shopping
Leisure/Travel Information

*Source: NOP "Women on the Web" January 2001

Hot Tips – Your e-mail program

- Make the most of the reply and forward features on your e-mail, the quickest way to get mail out

- Use cc and bcc to copy people in on an e-mail. Cc them if you don't mind them seeing the rest of the addressees, bcc if it's confidential

- Use your address book facility to store e-mail addresses so you don't have to remember (and type them in)

- Attach files to your e-mails as the quickest and fastest way to move documents. However, beware of viruses, which can be carried in attachments you receive on your e-mail. If you're not sure, always check the source of the e-mail before opening

- Customise your e-mails with a signature, which is automatically included on the bottom of your messages

- Write your e-mail offline (when you're not connected to the internet) and save your phone bills. Just log on and send them when you're ready

- Attach a return receipt to important e-mails, so that you know when they have arrived and been read

- AVOID USING BLOCK CAPITALS! This is viewed as the equivalent of online shouting, and is rude! Good manners are expected online, so it's important to know how to behave

Guide to e-mail addresses

E-mail addresses are made up of two elements, the username and the domain name, separated by the @ sign. Your username is the part of the address unique to you and the domain name is the address of your e-mail service provider. So if you have a Freeserve account, for example, your address will be you@freeserve.co.uk You can use any name you want as a user name, so it's fun to make up a name like **gorgeousMe@freeserve.co.uk.** At popular e-mail sites like **www.hotmail.com,** your name may already be in use by someone else with the same name! You could find yourself being the 51st Sarah Smith, with an e-mail address SarahSmith51@hotmail.com, or you could try playing around with nicknames until you find something unique.

Case Study
Norma Herdson

Norma Herdson, aged 61, from Maidenhead in Berkshire, who is a part-time Education Consultant, uses e-mail every day and the web several times a week for work related research. She says, "E-mail allows me to keep up-to-date with office stuff from home. It also means I can look at websites related to my profession. On two occasions I have brought up-to-date education information to my manager's attention. E-mail is also brilliant for keeping in touch with some friends in Central Europe – in the Czech Republic and Poland in particular."

Getting started

If you have access to the internet, you can use e-mail. All you'll need is an e-mail program and an e-mail address. You should have e-mail software included in your internet browser, but if not, you can get it from the net by downloading. Among the most popular e-mail programs are Outlook Express, Eudora, and Netscape's Messenger. All are equally straightforward to use and work in a similar way. Download programs from **http://officeupdate.microsoft.com**, and **www.eudora.com**.

Your Internet Service Provider (ISP) should automatically provide you with at least one e-mail address, and normally it's free, or included in your service charge. Your ISP will give you all the information you need to set up, or configure, an e-mail account.

Case Study
Sarah Green

"When I first used the net I never really knew what I was supposed to be doing or trying to achieve – I felt a need to understand it and to be 'online' but always seemed to browse around without a sense of purpose.

"Then things changed and whenever I needed to find something out – normally stuff relating to my home life more than my work life, it really started to work for me.

"If you include e-mail as a part of the web then it made a total difference to me – I actually e-mailed my (now) husband to ask him out to lunch!

"It's strange but I kind of have two groups of friends and family now – those who I communicate with online or on e-mail and those who are not yet connected! We like to send each other links to interesting websites.

"I think women have a completely different style of communication to men online – as they still keep emotion and expression in their communications where as men seem to get straight to the point – which I can sometimes find a bit abrupt."

Webmail – e-mail on the move!

Even if you don't have your own internet connection (and plan to use the internet at places like cybercafes and your local library) you can still get your own e-mail address, using webmail. Your e-mail messages will be stored on the internet at a central site, which you can access from anywhere. Wherever you are – at work, at home or on holiday – you can stay in touch via e-mail. Webmail is very convenient, and it's free. Once you go to a webmail site, it only takes a few minutes to get an account set up, and you have it for life. One of the most popular and easy to use webmail sites is Microsoft's **www.hotmail.com** – it seems like almost everyone has a Hotmail account, even if they only use it when they go on holiday! Other popular webmail sites include **www.yahoo.com**, **www.bigfoot.com** and **www.nameplanet.com**.

Sending an e-mail

Sending an e-mail is similar to sending a letter, and just as straightforward. You simply put the e-mail address of the person you're writing to in the 'To' field, complete the 'Subject' heading and write your message. You include any attachments, such as documents, photographs or other files and press 'Send'. When your e-mail arrives, your name, the subject and the date of the e-mail will all be displayed in the browser window of the addressee's e-mail inbox. They click on it to open it, and your full message is displayed.

How to create your own signature

Most e-mail programs let you insert your own 'Signature' at the bottom of the message. This can be anything you want, from more information on who you are (name, address, job title, company name and contact numbers) to a joke or poem.

Emoticons

To help you express emotions when you're e-mailing someone – or to emphasise you're making a joke, use emoticons – fun little icons meant to represent a human face. These are the most popular ones; or try making up your own!

:-)	Smiling
:-D	Laughing
:-(	Unhappy
;-)	Winking
:-P	Sticking out your tongue
O:-)	Angel
}:>	Devil
:'- (	Crying

Go to **www.emoticonuniverse.com** to find an unlimited number of emoticons!

Attaching and sending files

You can attach many types of files to your e-mail. Simply click on the 'Attach' icon and a list of the directories on your computer will appear. All you have to do is select the file you want to attach. When you go back to your message, it will have an 'Attach' heading which contains the icon, the name and the size of the file.

Once you've been using e-mail for a while, you might start to receive a lot of e-mails which have been forwarded on to you from your friends, called viral e-mails. These are generally joke e-mails, but they can also be virus warnings or chain letters, which may have films or pictures attached to them. You might want to forward the e-mail yourself, to all your friends' inboxes, and they, in turn, will forward them on. E-mails like this tend to spread extremely fast as people forward them around the world. When you receive attachments, it pays to be wary, as most computer viruses are transmitted this way. If you're not sure who has sent you something or what the attachment is, don't open it until you've found out. Viruses, like last summer's 'iloveyou' virus, can be fatal for your computer – the iloveyou virus wiped out computer systems around the world in a few hours. For more information on viruses, and how to avoid them, see the chapter on *Surfing Safely*.

Some useful guidelines

The very nature of e-mail – that it is so quick – has meant that most people use it as a brief and informal way of communication. When it comes to any kind of delicate negotiation, e-mail is not recommended – telephone or face to face contact is still crucial when it comes to emotive communication.

E-mail etiquette is another important matter. Although e-mail has the immediacy of a phone call, it has the permanency of a letter. It's best not to fire off angry or impulsive e-mails in the heat of the moment – this is called flaming, and you're sure to regret doing it!

The disadvantage of e-mail is that senders expect a quick response to their message because they know that you should have received the message within seconds of them sending it. You will also find that e-mails quickly mount up on your system – especially if you sign up for any of the information or bulletin services. It is well worth dealing with them straight away – either by filing them into appropriate 'Mailboxes' on the system or by deleting them as soon as you've read them.

Something else to bear in mind is that when you are e-mailing someone, you must get their e-mail address absolutely correct, otherwise it won't reach them. Most e-mail addresses are case sensitive, meaning you have to get the capitalization right, and be wary of dots and hyphens in the wrong place. If you make a mistake in the address, your e-mail might be 'bounced' back to you with an error message, so that you know it hasn't been delivered.

Spam, or junk e-mail

Like snail mail, once you've had your e-mail address for a while, you will start to get junk e-mails, also called Spam, sent with annoying regularity into your inbox. They are normally commercial messages, like ads, and are fairly harmless. However, they can sometimes be more disturbing, so it pays to be careful. Once you start receiving Spam, there's not much you can do to stop getting it. **www.mail-abuse.org** is an anti-Spam campaigning website. Log on to join the fight against Spam!

The more exposure your e-mail address gets (for example, using it for contact details when you buy something from the web), the more junk mail you'll get. There may be an 'unsubscribe' option on the junk e-mail, which should help cut down on the amount your receive. It is possible to buy filtering software to eliminate some junk mail, but it's often ineffective. Try **www.junkbusters.com** to find out more about how to stop junk mail and other invasions of your privacy.

One solution is to use two e-mail addresses – use one purely for activities where you give out your e-mail address to strangers (for example, on other websites) and one for personal use.

See the chapter on *Surfing Safely* to find out more about your privacy and the internet.

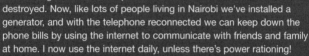

Case Study
Erin Knowles

"The internet for me personally is vital. I live in Kenya with my husband but our two daughters live and work in London. Communications here are very difficult and incredibly expensive. This year, for example, we have experienced daily power rationing due to the drought. When the rains finally came a large amount of telephone wires were destroyed. Now, like lots of people living in Nairobi we've installed a generator, and with the telephone reconnected we can keep down the phone bills by using the internet to communicate with friends and family at home. I now use the internet daily, unless there's power rationing!

"The internet is the most amazing invention. What I've found on it so far has really only been the tip of the iceberg, but I'm excited to know that the information available is almost infinite. Therefore no matter where my interests lie, and no matter how remote I am, the internet will be my reference at the click of a button! My favourite sites on the internet are **www.amazon.com** and **www.handbag.com** – I can buy everything I need and get it sent to me out here!"

Finding an e-mail address

Unfortunately, there is no universal directory of e-mail addresses. If you need to find someone, work your way through the e-mail search sites listed at the end of this chapter. If you want people to be able to find your address, register with those same sites, but be aware they are the main source of Spam. People-finding sites, like **www.whowhere.com** are very simple to use. It's just a matter of typing in the details of the person you're trying to find (such as their name and the country they live in) and the site will hopefully come up with their e-mail address, or even their address and phone number.

Instant Messaging

Similar to e-mail, except quicker, Instant Messaging enables you to send short messages which arrive the moment you send them. You can chat to your friends in real time, and the program will alert you when they log on, so that you can send them a message. There are a number of free Instant Messaging programs to download – if your friends already use one, use theirs, because at the moment the programs are not compatible. The two most popular are AIM, from AOL, and ICQ (I seek you). Download them from **www.icq.com** and **http://free.aol.com/aim** or see the main list of Instant Messaging sites at the end of this chapter.

Case Study
Julia Jacques

"I've been using the MSN Messenger service as well as the AOL 'live chat' service for about six months now. Everyone at work uses Messenger, so it's an ideal way of chatting or sending a quick message in complete privacy, and without the formality of an e-mail.

"The programmes let you know when friends are logged on, and you can exchange instant messages, like mini e-mails, either one- to-one or as a group. It's great for chatting to mates who are travelling or living abroad, and if you're both sat on computers with microphones you can chat just as if you were on the phone!

"It can be a bit of a pain if you're receiving messages constantly, but you can 'block' people, or show your status as being offline if you don't wish to be disturbed while you're working. I find it really useful for quick questions at work, or arranging a night out with friends – it's quicker than a phone call and you can chat to more than one person at the same time."

Mailing Lists

Mailing lists are like e-mail newsletters, a simple way to receive regular updates and information from the internet. There are thousands of mailing lists out there running discussions between list subscribers on an infinite number of subjects – subscribe to one and you'll get newsletters and updates sent to your inbox regularly. The best way to find and join a list is to log onto one of the mailing list directories, which will also walk you through the subscribing process. Try **www.liszt.com** or **www.coollist.com.** You can even start your own mailing list, at **www.egroups.com**.

Wherever you are, at work, at home or on holiday, you can stay in touch with e-mail.

You know it's time to log on when:

- You want the latest news delivered to your desktop
- You want to stay in touch with friends wherever you are in the world
- You want to update colleagues on a work project

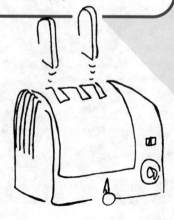

E-mail websites

Webmail sites

www.hotmail.com is the original free webmail service. It has one of the best Spam blocking systems and the bonus of an Instant Messaging service.

All the major portals now offer free e-mail, so you can get an account while you're there and keep everything in the same place. **www.yahoo.com** and **www.handbag.com** both offer free e-mail among their many services.

www.chickmail.com is a webmail site connected to the feisty chickclick portal.

www.twigger.co.uk has free e-mail forwarding for anyone with an e-mail address from a British provider – get your mail sent to the most convenient inbox.

www.nameplanet.com gives you your name as an e-mail address e.g. james@smith.net, for free!

www.bigfoot.com is a new take on webmail – it will forward your mail to the e-mail address you are actually currently using, no matter how many times your location or job changes. It also blocks Spam, sends you reminders and replies to your mail while you're away!

www.postmaster.co.uk specialises in privacy and will not sell your e-mail address to anyone, with a strict no-Spam policy. Similar security-based sites are **www.hushmail.com** and **www.ziplip.com**.

www.emailaddresses.com is a US directory of the thousands of free webmail providers.

www.another.com, gives you the chance to choose your own domain name (e.g. you@onstrike.co.uk) from a massive selection of phrases – and get a name that speaks volumes about you!

www.purpleturtle.com sends 20% of their advertising revenue to help endangered species. Do your bit to save the environment with minimal effort!

General e-mail resources

www.mailround.com will help you earn points and make your e-mails look more interesting, using stamps supporting advertising in the mail you send and receive.

www.zaplet.com is a great site with e-mail tools you can use to send to groups of friends or colleagues.

www.anonymizer.com and **www.uboot.com** enable you to send anonymous e-mail, if you're so inclined.

Finding people online

http://people.scoot.co.uk will enable you to find e-mail addresses, telephone numbers and street addresses of over 17 million people in the UK!

www.atchoo.org/search.html is the fastest way to find someone's university e-mail address – all students are provided with an e-mail address by their university.

www.whowhere.com
www.peoplesite.com
www.bigfoot.com
www.excite.com
www.altavista.com
www.four11.com
www.people.yahoo.com
www.iaf.net

Instant Messaging sites

www.icq.com will give you a downloadable instant messaging program to send messages to the other 20 million ICQ users in the world.

http://free.aol.com/aim will enable you to get AOL's instant messaging program. All AOL users automatically have this, that's over 20 million people!

http://messenger.yahoo.com is the place to download Yahoo! messenger.

http://messenger.msn.com runs in conjunction with Hotmail, so if your friends mostly have Hotmail addresses, this is your best bet for keeping in touch with them.

Mailing lists

www.lizst.com is a search engine dedicated to mailing lists, so you'll easily be able to find one that interests you.

www.topica.com is a free internet service which enables you to find and participate in e-mail mailing lists, and manage your lists easily.

www.daytips.com has free daily newsletters and e-zines sent to your inbox, on a variety of different subjects.

www.egroups.com is Yahoo's group e-mail service – helps you connect to others who share your ideas.

www.coollist.com is an easy way to get free mailing list services.

Chapter 4

Searching the Internet

The best thing about the internet is the huge amount of information it contains – over 1 billion pages and growing exponentially. However, its size can also be one of its main drawbacks. Sometimes it is like searching for a needle in a billion haystacks, which can be overwhelming!

One of the most important internet skills to have is to be able to search for something quickly and accurately. Unless you are good at searching, you won't be making the most of the internet. The good news is, it's not too hard to grasp the basics, and with a little practice you'll soon be an expert.

The most-used way of finding something on the internet is to use a search tool, a site that specialises in searching the whole of the net for what you tell it to look for. It will then present you with the results of its search, which hopefully will contain what you were looking for. It's worth bearing in mind that search sites can't possibly keep up with the incredible growth of the net – it is estimated that less than 20% of the net is indexed at any one time. The key to a successful search is to try different combinations of search terms and search engines – if at first, you don't succeed, keep trying and you're sure to come across what you're looking for.

Types of search tools

There are many different kinds of search tool, which all search the net in different ways. Understanding how each one works will help you decide the best way to go about a search.

Search indexes aim to cover every single piece of information on every net page in existence – a huge task! This means you have to ensure your search terms are as accurate as possible, otherwise you'll be faced with an overwhelming amount of irrelevant information. The best known of the indexes is probably **www.altavista.com**, which is also fairly user-friendly. The advantage of indexes is that they are larger and fresher than other search tools, but they can be unwieldy. For tips on improving the accuracy of your searches on indexes, see the Hot Tips section later in the chapter.

Search directories are compiled by real people, and are better if you just want to browse a range of sites in a particular area, rather than find anything specific. It will have a selection of links you can keep clicking through, as you narrow down your search to find what you want. The most famous of these is **www.yahoo.com**, which also comes with a specialised UK directory, at **www.yahoo.co.uk**. Yahoo! like many search engines, also has additional content like news, shopping and e-mail so that you've got everything you need in one place. There are also specialist directories on the net; **www.femina.com** is a specialised directory for women. The advantage of a search directory is that it is more organised, because humans put it together, but does not cover as much of the net as an index.

Metasearch sites will search a range of search engines and sites for you simultaneously, and compile a final list, filtered for accuracy. This will save you having to search each engine individually for what you want. Try **www.google.com** or **www.dogpile.com** for a good start.

Search assistants are one of the most user-friendly ways to search the net. You generally just type in a question, and it will come back with a range of links and results from other search engines, with all the possible answers to your question. The most fun of these is **www.askjeeves.com** and **www.askjeeves.co.uk**, who will help you with any question you ask. You can even see what questions other users are asking!

One way to find something specific (for example, a corporate site) is to try guessing at its internet address. If you are looking for the site of a company called Smith's, you could try typing in **www.smiths.com** in your browser bar. If it is a UK company, the web address is likely to end with .co.uk, like **www.smiths.co.uk**. Other common endings are .net, .org, .org.uk, .gov.uk. You'll soon know if the address is not right.

Hot Tips – Using search engines

All the different kinds of search engines operate similarly, so once you have the hang of using one, you can easily master the others.

1 To start, type a searching keyword (whatever you want to look up) into the search box on the search engine, and click on 'Search'

2 On an index site, like **www.altavista.com**, you'll get a list of links to pages containing that keyword. The list will be very long, but it will be listed by relevancy, so what you're looking for will ideally be near the top of the list. Index sites are good for specific searches, especially when you know all the short cuts!

3 On a directory site, like **www.yahoo.com**, typing in the keyword will return you a list of related categories, which you then use to narrow down your search until you get to the site or information you're looking for. Using a directory is better if you have a general idea of what you're looking for – you can just browse around until you find it

4 To save time, you could try a metasearch tool like **www.metacrawler.com**, which searches all the search engines simultaneously and collects the results for you

If at first you don't find what you're looking for, don't give up! Try a different type of search engine, or use a metasearcher, or refine your search terms to make them more accurate.

Becoming a searching pro

If you can't find what you're looking for, or your search results are too large; it's worth refining your search terms so that the search engine knows exactly what you're looking for. Each search engine has slightly different rules for you to do this, so it's worth looking it up on the site itself to get handy hints on making your search more accurate. However, certain general rules work on most sites..

For example, if you're looking up Jamie Oliver recipes on the internet, the most obvious way to start would be to type Jamie Oliver in the search window. However, you would then get back a huge list of all sites containing the words Jamie or Oliver, which may not have anything related to the Naked Chef at all. To save you reading through the entire list, which could take a week, it's worth refining your search.

- To search for pages containing the words Jamie and Oliver, type a plus sign in front of each word: +jamie +oliver. Or, depending on the search engine's rules, type Jamie AND Oliver

- Similarly, you can use a minus sign to eliminate words you don't want in the search, or just type NOT

- To get a list of pages containing the words Jamie and Oliver written together, put the words in quotation marks, so that you are searching for a phrase: 'Jamie Oliver'

- Use an asterisk, or wildcard, towards the ending of a word, to search for variations of that word – for example, 'Jamie Oliver' cook* will search for cook, cookery, cooking,etc

These are just the basic rules, but it's well worth getting the hang of them to save time searching for what you want. The biggest search sites, like **www.altavista.com** and **www.dmoz.com**, all have their own help pages which are worth looking at to find out even more about advanced searching.

Case Study
Kirstin Davies

Kirstin, a 23 year-old conference producer, says:
"I really don't know how I got by before the internet!
I use it every day and in all aspects of my life –
everything from work-related research to booking
concert tickets. When I first started surfing, it took
me a long time to find what I needed. I was quite
unsure about how to use a search engine, so I
tended just to go to the sites whose addresses I already
knew. When I did try searching a directory, I used to get an
overwhelming list of irrelevant links, and it was impossible to find what I
was looking for! I soon realised, however, that I wasn't using the internet
to its fullest potential, so I decided to improve my searching skills. A
couple of hours finding my way around Yahoo! at **www.yahoo.com** and
Alta Vista at **www.altavista.com**, learning the different searching
shortcuts, meant I quickly found what I was looking for every time. Both
sites have great help pages as well, in case you get stuck. It's worth
spending the time getting the hang of searching – you'll save so much
more time in the long run! I now use most of the search engines
regularly, (my favourite is **www.google.com** because it seems the most
accurate) and I have even customised my Yahoo! page so it shows
exactly the information I want!"

You know it's time to log on when:

- You want to access the world's biggest library from home
- You want to make learning more fun

Searching the web

Search sites

www.alltheweb.com – with 575 million URLs listed, this is currently the biggest search index on the internet, and is fairly simple to use.

www.ditto.com is a unique index searching for images rather than text.

www.altavista.com is the most well-known index on the internet; its help pages are also good.

www.euroseek.net searches the net from a European perspective, and even includes multi-lingual searching.

www.god.co.uk is a British search site.

www.hotbot.com and **www.hotbot.co.uk** are both long-running indexes.

www.lycos.com and **www.lycos.co.uk** are known for their MP3 searches.

www.infoseek.co.uk has a good range of search results.

www.raging.com is one of the newer indexes, and is quick and easy to use.

www.go.com – owned by Disney, this returns youth-oriented search results.

www.google.com is one of the most popular search indexes on the net, with impressive, easy-to-use features.

Web directories

www.yahoo.com and **www.yahoo.co.uk** should be your first search stop on the net. Yahoo! has so many features it's become a portal, and using their category-based search results makes everything easier. You can search the whole net, or just for UK-based sites.

www.dmoz.com is the home of the Open Directory, which is edited by over 40,000 volunteers keeping it as up to date as possible!

www.excite.co.uk is a big directory with UK specific content.

www.looksmart.com and **www.looksmart.co.uk** both have comprehensive listings.

www.northernlight.com is one of the biggest US search directories.

www.ukplus.co.uk lets you focus your search on UK sites only. Similar UK sites include **www.ukdirectory.co.uk**, **www.ukmax.co.uk**, and **www.ukonline.co.uk**.

www.yell.com is the Yellow Pages online – faster and less bulky than the offline version!

www.scoot.co.uk has all kinds of local information.

www.about.com is a friendly, interests-based directory.

Metasearches

www.askjeeves.com, **www.askjeeves.co.uk** and **www.ajkids.com** will provide you with a comprehensive set of results, searching web directories, indexes and keywords. It's fun to use – just type in any question and see what Jeeves can come up with!

www.metacrawler.com will search the search engines on your behalf.

www.copernic.com searches the main search sites, and removes any duplication in your results.

www.mirago.com is a UK-based metasearch engine.

www.mamma.com claims to be the biggest metasearch engine on the net.

www.dogpile.com

www.savvysearch.com

www.alloversearch.com

Specialist directories

www.femina.com is a specialist directory for women's sites.
www.wwwomen.com is another long-running search directory for women, returning female-oriented results.
www.directoryguide.com and **www.searchengineguide.com** are search directories of specialist search directories – they'll help you find the directory for your area of interest.

Other resources

www.searchenginewatch.com is a site that has current ratings for search engines, as well as user tips and reviews.
www.searchengineshowdown.com has current rankings for all major search sites.
www.searchiq.com is a guide to the main search sites.

Surfing Safely

Like most things in life, it's best to take a few precautions and safety steps when surfing – think of them as your online safety belt. With a few smart moves you can keep the big, bad, and ugly out of your computer.

There are lots of options available to make surfing a lot safer for you and your family. It's just up to you to decide what services and information you want to make available and what you want to block. To make the journey into cyberspace a happy one it's also useful to sit down and talk through some safety guidelines with the family, so that everyone is aware of the potential dangers and how to avoid them.

Kids, especially, can be very trusting of strangers they meet on the internet, so it's best to go over the rules before you let them loose on the net! Surfing safely is simply a matter of common sense – just like being safe in the real world!

Privacy

The internet gives companies the opportunity to get a lot of personal information on you, which they then use for commercial ends, to try and sell you more products. For example, you may have to register to use a site, giving information like your name, age and address. Chances are, this information won't be used for anything more sinister than marketing – but you can control how much detail you want to give them. Reputable sites may have a box you can tick when you register, to opt-in or opt-out of having any personal information used or passed on. Kids are often too happy to give away this type of information in return for being sent products, so it's important to make sure they know what is and what is not acceptable to you. Find out more at **www.dataprotection.gov.uk**.

If you use the internet and e-mail at work, it's worth bearing in mind that your employer has the legal right to access your e-mail and internet files – you have no right to privacy as an employee. To make sure you don't get into any trouble, find out what your employer's policies are. In some cases, people have lost their jobs for sending inappropriate e-mails to their colleagues from their work e-mail addresses. Similarly, your company is able to track how much time you are spending online and which sites you're accessing. If you're spending all day booking a holiday instead of working, you might get caught!

Even on your own computer, your browser automatically keeps a record of the sites you've accessed recently, in the 'History' file. You may want to delete this file if you don't want anyone seeing where you've been surfing. Find out more about your employment rights and the internet at **www.dti.gov.uk/er**.

Other people

Chatting online is a fun way to meet new people. However, it pays to take precautions whenever you interact with strangers on the net. This includes in chat rooms and forums, online clubs, and newsgroups. You might accidentally come across someone you'd rather not be in contact with. It's possible to block other people from being able to send you emails and chat messages, depending on your e-mail software. If you're still being pestered, you can contact that person's ISP to report their bad behaviour – they'll be warned, and may even be cut off from the internet altogether! For more information check out **www.chatdanger.com**.

Hot Tips – Online safety

- Guard your anonymity: don't give out any personal details, unless it's to someone you know well enough to trust
- Never reveal your passwords, even if someone official sounding asks for them; there's no reason anyone else needs your password
- Listen to your gut instincts when dealing with strangers online; if you feel something isn't wise or safe, it probably isn't
- If you do decide to meet up with someone you've met on the net, make sure you take a friend and meet up in a public place. It might help to talk on the phone first to get more of an idea of the person
- If you're worried about the content your kids will view online, then restrict access to unsuitable sites using the preferences on your browser program

Shopping safely

Shopping on the net is no riskier than shopping on
your local high street, although it may feel less secure
because of the smaller amount of human interaction. It takes a certain
amount of trust to give out your credit card details to a machine, but really
it's no more dangerous than handing it to someone behind a counter.
However, there are certain safety issues associated with e-commerce.
Log on to the Office of Fair Trading at **www.oft.gov.uk** to find out more.

It's best to only shop at sites you trust – big internet brand names,
or high street shops. Smaller operations may be operating some kind
of scam. You could try looking up the company's address at
www.dotcomdirectory.com. Most of the reputable e-commerce sites
are rated by consumer groups, and will have a seal of approval on their
websites. These include the TRUSTe seal **www.truste.org**, the Better
Business Bureau at **www.bbbonline.com**, and Verisign at
www.verisign.com.

It's important to switch to a secure connection before you actually type in
your credit card details to buy something. Secure mode means any
information sent between your computer and the site is encrypted, so no
one else can understand it if they are hacking in. Most sites automatically
switch over into secure mode when it's time to pay, and your browser will
also send you an alert message to let you know when you are joining or
leaving secure mode. If in doubt, there should be a little key or padlock
icon along the bottom bar of your browser window when you are secure.
A secure web page's web address will always begin with https:// rather
than http://

Once you've made an order, keep a record of it for future reference in
case anything goes wrong with the delivery.

Although sites offer alternative methods of payment, it's still best to use
a credit card so that any liability goes to the card company if your details
are stolen. Check your individual credit card for its rules regarding
fraudulent usage.

Steve Newman is the Information Communication and Technology (ICT) teacher at Presdales School in Hertfordshire, a 1000-pupil girls' comprehensive school with sixth form. Upon achieving Language College status in 1996, the school decided to focus on developing the use of ICT in its foreign language teaching. It is believed to be the only project of its kind in the UK.

"Security and safety is an important issue " he explains: "We want to protect the girls from accessing unsuitable sites. The internet service is provided and managed by the local county council. Certain words for searching are banned and the web addresses are filtered. And on the whole this is successful. We also have a signed contract with all pupils and their parents or guardians. This ensures that all parties know the do's and don'ts of internet access in the school."

Hannah Ellison is a Year 13 pupil at Presdales: "Having internet access at school has made accessing up to date information easy. It is a really useful research tool for school projects and coursework. The school's policies make the pupils responsible for their own internet use and they have worked with us to modify the rules on what we can and can't access. The level of control is made suitable for each year group and as I have progressed up the school I have been given more freedom."

Kids' safety on the net

As we know, although there's a lot of content on the net that is perfect for kids, there's also a lot we would prefer they didn't see. There are ways of restricting kids' access to inappropriate sites, but none of them are foolproof, and kids' advanced computer skills mean they can probably get around them themselves.

Depending on your browser, you'll be able to set different content filters on what can be accessed, so that you can bar sites with unsuitable content. There are different levels of ratings – you can block bad language, nudity, violence and sexual content. Just access the 'Options' setting on your menu bar and put the settings as you see fit. Sites rated like this all belong to one standard, set by the World Wide Web consortium. This ratings standard, called PICS (Platform for Internet Content Selection), can be accessed at **www.w3.org/PICS** for more information.

There are also a wide number of software filters which you can install on your computer, which help to control kids' internet access. They tend to filter using keywords to block unsuitable material, but, again they are not unbeatable! However, it's well worth looking into installing software if your kids are confirmed net heads, as filters are improving all the time. Try **www.netnanny.com** or see the full listings of different filtering programs below.

Whatever you use to control what your kids can access, it's important still to keep an eye on what they get up to online, to make sure they're behaving responsibly. Better safe than sorry!

Despite all the news hype, the internet is no more dangerous than the real world. It's important just to bear these guidelines in mind before you start surfing, but, with a bit of commonsense, nothing bad will come of your net experiences.

You know it's time to log on when:

• You want to stop your kids seeing too much on the net
• You want to take sensible precautions before joining a chatroom

Safety sites

General safety resources

www.internetwatch.org.uk is a great site from the Internet Watch Foundation formed to address the problem of illegal material on the internet, especially child pornography.
www.rsac.org is the homepage of the Internet Content Rating Association.
www.w3.org is the homepage of the World Wide Web consortium, formed to promote best practices and International Web Standards.
www.scambusters.com is a site detailing all the scams on the internet, with virus updates, Spam guards, and details of popular credit card frauds.
www.worldwidescam.com is a huge resource listing all the big internet fraud schemes, worth looking at simply for interest.
www.antivirus.about.com is a huge resource for finding out all about computer viruses, including the crucial information on how to avoid them.
www.about.com is a mine of useful information on computing generally.
www.vmyths.com is where to learn about virus myths, hoaxes and urban legends, so that you're never taken in again!
www.childnet–int.org has resources to make the net safe for kids.

Privacy sites

www.dataprotection.gov.uk is the homepage for the Commissioner for Data Protection – an independent supervisory authority protecting consumers' right to privacy.
www.epic.org is the homepage of the Electronic Privacy Information Center, a US organisation working for protecting privacy rights on the net.
www.mail-abuse.org is an anti-Spam campaigning website.
www.junkbusters.com offers you tips on cutting down the amount of Spam you receive.

Filtering software

www.netnanny.com is one of the best-known filtering programs for kids, to give you better control over what your kids can get up to online – you can track everyone's online activities and even log and record all chat sessions. Buy the program directly from the site, or just find out about how it works.

www.surfcontrol.com is the home of the Cybercontrol program for school and home internet access control. Download a free trial from the site.

www.cybersitter.com is another popular filtering/blocking program with a free trial version available.

www.surfmonkey.com is a browser program designed for kids, with its own chat channels

Shopping safely

www.oft.gov.uk is the homepage of the Office of Fair Trading – find out about your consumer rights.

www.bizrate.com has an online marketplace of approved traders, or you can check on a site to find out how trustworthy it is.

www.which.net runs the Which? Webtrader scheme. Companies can display the Which? Webtrader logo on their website in return for complying with the Which code of practice, endeavouring to treat consumers fairly.

www.ilevel.com is a US site which mediates disputes between consumers and retailers.

www.isitsafe.com is the homepage of the Internet Consumer Assistance Bureau.

Chapter 6

Portals – Your Gateway to the Net

The beauty of the internet is that whatever you need, there will be a site, or sites, to help you out. But, with such an overwhelming amount of information, it can be difficult to know where to start, especially if you are new to surfing. This is where portal sites come in.

One of the best ways to start your internet journey is to head for a site called a portal. Portals act like a directory of information, providing a gateway to the net as well as a useful resource for specific areas like health, sport or women – the source of a wealth of information, contacts and internet tools. There are all kinds of portals, specialising in different areas, and useful for different functions. Sites like **www.yahoo.co.uk**, **www.msn.co.uk** and **www.freeserve.com** offer a range of general content like news and e-mail access. There are also special-interest portals like **www.moonfruit.com**, where you can create your own net community!

Once you've found a portal you like, it may be worth setting it as your homepage, so that you always start your surfing from that portal. Similarly, one of the most useful features of many portals is that they are customisable, so you can set them up to show exactly the information you need. For example, creating your own 'myBBC' site at **www.bbc.co.uk** gives you access to a wide range of content such as news and TV guides. Customising sites in this way can help you feel more at home, and makes any surfing you do much quicker, because the site will be edited for what you need – there'll be nothing irrelevant to you on your site! You set your own preferences, so that you're shown information like the weather forecast in your area or even local cinema times. Typically, you'll be able to get all the entertainment, travel, and business news that you need, as well as other fun features like a personalised greeting or daily horoscope!

Women's portals

The massive rise in the number of women accessing the net has encouraged the creation of some high profile portals that focus entirely on women's lifestyles.

While every portal is different, with its own unique approach and target market, the main purpose of female-focused portals is to provide everything a busy woman could need, in one place. You can find out about the latest fashions and recipes, read saucy sex tips or discuss relationship problems. You'll find news, shopping and horoscopes, chatrooms and how-to guides covering everything from car maintenance to childcare. Most have bulletin boards and mailing lists as well as search directories, to help you find a particular service, product or piece of information.

The biggest women's portals, like **www.handbag.com**, **www.beme.com**, and **www.ivillage.co.uk,** offer the sort of content you would expect in your favourite magazine and more. With the added benefit of interactivity, you get a real depth of information and links. These new portals provide a place to exchange information and be part of a cohesive and mutually supportive community of women.

Leading UK portals and websites

1. www.MSN.com
2. www.yahoo.com
3. www.microsoft.com
4. www.freeserve.com
5. www.msn.co.uk
6. www.passport.com
7. www.yahoo.co.uk
8. www.bbc.co.uk
9. www.lycos.com
10. www.btinternet.com

MMXI Top 10 Domains in the UK, November 2000

"I try and look into the discussion boards daily on **www.handbag.com**, and especially at the weekends in my free time. It surprised me how involved I feel – you get reeled in. I went into participating on the boards cautiously, but now I can't keep away!

"I also like to look into the agony aunt letters and replies, I do the competitions, and if something catches my eye on the front page as I enter the site, especially if it's a free offer, then I might check that out first. I've had access to the internet for about a year and discovered **www.handbag.com** when I was looking for some advice about a personal problem that I felt I couldn't speak to anyone about. I do find the site easy to use and it satisfies all my internet needs. I have found that virtual friends can really get to you – you can feel passionately for people you have never met, and I find myself really wanting to try to help them and try to give participants some advice. In discussions online it's not like when you go into a room full of people and you might be the 'quiet one', there is a real friendliness and sense of community, and the feeling that everyone is equal."

With so many time pressures and demands on us already, it makes sense to find a site relevant to your life and use it time and time again. In this highly competitive market, the main players offer very strong content and have established commercial partnerships which enable highly attractive deals on products and services. At present, the women's portals make the majority of their revenue from advertising and sponsorship, but shopping is growing, with women buying more groceries, books and clothes online than ever before. No wonder women's portals are proving one of the internet's greatest success stories and attracting male as well as female surfers from all walks of life.

Web facts - Portals

* The average internet user is very loyal and, once they have found a portal they like, will return to it again and again

* Women are responsible for the majority of household spending decisions, from mortgages to holidays. Women's portals often have strong content on consumer issues, and can be a great help!

* Internet destinations for women focus on what women need: time and money-saving tips, lifestyle information, shopping, advice and entertainment

* Although targeting women of all ages, visitors to women's portals tend to be busy women in their 30s

* UK women's sites are highly competitive, with new partnerships and content deals being struck by all the main portals

* **www.ivillage.co.uk** is the UK version of the US women's portal **www.ivillage.com**, in partnership with the Tesco supermarket chain

* **www.handbag.com** was the first of the UK women's portals, attracting 312,000 visitors per month, co-owned by Boots and Hollinger Telegraph New Media

The portals

It is early days for the women's portal market in the UK and there is intensive competition. All the sites are fighting to attract a loyal audience. So, which one is right for you?

Women want the internet to be useful, just like their handbag, which is the proposition behind **www.handbag.com**. It provides information on women's specific interests, from health, beauty, fashion and shopping to personal finance, careers, motoring and property. With women making the majority of household spending decisions, it is good to see a site that reflects this.

www.handbag.com also offers a range of internet services, from e-mail and free net access to phone books and directories. The site also answers your beauty queries together with reviews of cosmetics and top selling beauty products.

A new entrant from the US, where its counterpart **www.ivillage.com** had six million visitors in June 2000, the hugely successful **www.ivillage.co.uk** is here loud and clear.

A home-grown site worth trying is **www.beme.com** - the 'first place for women on the web' with a magazine feel to it – using IPC content with strong e-commerce tie-ins.

With message boards, instant messaging and chatrooms, **www.femail.co.uk** lives up to its offline counterpart, the 'femail' pages of the Daily Mail.

While some portals have a distinctly commercial feel, **www.everywoman.co.uk**, founded in September 1999, has a friendly, approachable woman-to-woman atmosphere. Designed to help women balance work and home life, it launched the UK's first online workforce and offers some great business and home community advice. It currently has thirteen channels, or subject areas, ranging from law to horoscopes.

Brought to you by Freeserve, **www.icircle.com** provides services and advice from the experts. There's a fitness specialist, relationships counsellor, careers mentor and travel guide. It also has over 40 channels and content is updated daily.

US portals for women

It is also worth visiting some of the US sites that cover a wide range of topics in depth, such as **www.women.com**, which has made a big commitment to women's issues. Although topics like women's empowerment may not be the top of everyone's agenda, portals like this help us to open up the discussion of issues that affect women to a broader audience and provide a much-needed forum for debate.

www.chickclick.com is a US portal for younger women. It's quite sassy and opinionated, but fun as well.

Another good US portal for women is **www.oxygen.com**, partly-owned by Oprah Winfrey, this site focuses on spiritual well-being and happiness. It also links to a number of e-zines, electronic magazines, which are worth a look.

Women's portals offer a wide range of interesting and entertaining content and they draw a broad audience including lots of men! Backed by big investment, the coming year is set to see the leading sites offering even more in terms of content and e-commerce.

You know it's time to log on when:

- You're overwhelmed by the choice of the internet, and want to narrow it down to the essentials!
- You need to find information that's tailored to you
- You want to get the best deals on products

Women's portals

www.handbag.com has everything you need from your handbag.
www.ivillage.com and **www.ivillage.co.uk** have a great range of useful content.
www.beme.com is the 'first place for women on the web'.
www.femail.co.uk comes from the 'femail' pages of the Daily Mail.
www.everywoman.co.uk is a friendly, work-related women's portal.
www.icircle.com is Freeserve's women's portal.
www.women.com focuses on women's issues.
www.chickclick.com is a feisty US portal for younger women.
www.oxygen.com is an American internet network.

General portals

www.freeserve.com is Freeserve's home page, with features like searching, SMS text messaging and news listings.
www.msn.co.uk is Microsoft's portal, with a comprehensive range of features like e-mail and searching.
www.yahoo.co.uk is one of the most popular UK search sites, also offering e-mail, Instant Messaging and chat.
www.excite.co.uk is another good search engine which also acts as a portal.
www.zoom.co.uk is a fashion and lifestyle shopping portal, with links to a lot of high street brands.
www.open.gov.uk is a public sector portal, with links to all areas of Government.
www.about.com is a hobbies and leisure portal, containing a vast wealth of information in articles, links and other resources.
www.imdb.co.uk is the Internet Movie Database.
www.cnn.co.uk and **www.bbc.co.uk** are both big news sites, which are constantly updated with the latest stories.
www.schoolzone.co.uk is a good education portal.
www.netdoctor.co.uk is a good place to start your search for health content on the net.
www.moonfruit.com lets you create your own mini-site, or browse through others' creations, hosted for free by moonfruit.

Chapter 7

Web Networking

The internet has changed the way we communicate; more and more women are networking online, sharing ideas and experiences, developing connections, contacts and online relationships. Forget the old school tie and the old boys' network, the internet has created a whole new breed of non-elitist, testosterone-free networking groups and communities. Some are purely business-focused, others are just for fun, the choice is yours.

One of the easiest ways to network with others is to join an online chatroom. Anytime of the day or night you can chat to people on any subject from current affairs to more intimate subjects.

Paula Paul from Datchet, Berkshire finds the internet is a brilliant way to make new friends: "I have started making new friends on the internet via **www.icq.com**, an instant messaging system, and joined a chatroom for regular mind stretching quizzes and humourous conversation. You don't need to give your real name and no one needs to know anything about you unless you tell them."

Web Life – The art of online conversation

- Live chat. For immediate gratification visit a live chatroom and take part in live and honest chats in real time. Try **http://chat.yahoo.com**

- Moderated chat. Many chatrooms are moderated, which means the moderator checks the comments before they are released to view. These are ideal for kids. Try **www.schoolchat.co.uk**

- Internet Relay Chat (IRC). Talk to many people at once. Check out **www.mirc.co.uk** for instructions and software downloads, and see the list at the end of this chapter

- Instant Messages. Send a message to all your friends or chat one to one in real time. **www.icq.com** is one of the most popular programs. See the chapter on e-mail for more details about downloads

- Newsletters and bulletins straight to your inbox. For more information, see the chapter on e-mail, or log on to **www.liszt.com**

- Usenet newsgroups cover every issue you can think of. From messages and discussions to questions and answer, take a look at **www.deja.com**

It's the business

Women have often been a little sceptical about sharing business ideas and networking. We often can't afford the time or resources to spend time enlarging our circle of contacts. But the online women's business networks are changing all that. With no hidden agenda and a refreshingly informal atmosphere, they are attracting more and more like-minded women. Many have a professional focus, like **www.hightech-women.com**, yet are unthreatening and collaborative, with no hierarchical boundaries. Students and CEOs mix happily for mutual benefit, and enjoy mentoring and meeting.

Then there's First Tuesday at **www.firsttuesday.com**. Aimed at bringing investors and entrepreneurs together in Europe's largest forum, the meetings are large, hyperactive and focused on facilitating new business relations. For smaller meetings, check out **www.busygirl.co.uk** for entrepreneurial and corporate women. With monthly briefings on a whole host of business issues, this group has over 3,000 members.

Chatter boxes

If you're fed up with the TV or family smalltalk, you can log on and get chatting with people who share your interests. Women all over the world are making friends online, through chatrooms and women's user groups. Try out the chat areas on large portals like **www.yahoo.com**, to take part in some of the most popular chat sites, or look up **www.100hot.com/chat** for the latest listings of top ranked chat sites.

You can have a girlie chat about beauty tips, or a deep discussion of world politics; whatever your mood, you can find a discussion group on your wavelength. Many offer special features, such as the chance to create your own cartoon image of yourself. For a few laughs try the various chatrooms hosted by **www.funny.co.uk**.

When you enter a chatroom for the first time, it can be quite confusing – with more than one conversation going on around you, it's like standing in the middle of a party! You can just watch (called lurking), or join in as soon as you've got something to say. But whatever you do, make sure you know your netiquette!

Case Study
Janet Morrison

Janet, a 39 year old solicitor, heads the
e-business department she established
at Kerman & Co.

"I believe the internet is an invaluable networking
tool for women. Most of my business comes
from contacts made at networking events and
conferences, both virtual and in the 'real' world.
E-networking, websites and e-mail make it much easier for me to
develop and maintain good relationships with potential clients without
being too intrusive. The interactivity and immediacy of communication
enabled by the net.

A single parent with two school-aged children, and a high-flying career,
Janet encounters the same challenges many women face when trying
to balance their hectic lives. However, she has found that being able to
work from home has been a big help. She used the internet primarily as
a business tool supporting communication, organisation and availability.

"The principle benefit of the internet is its ability to save precious time.
Women managing a career and bringing up children have very little time
to spare, and anything that saves time is a bonus. The net is also a
tremendous research tool, and it's essential for keeping up-to-date with
changes in the rapidly evolving area of the Law I practice. I use websites
that filter news for me and deliver only information that is directly
relevant to myself and my clients."

"I am a 27 year old married mother of two young girls. I was diagnosed with Multiple Sclerosis in June 1999. I remain fairly fit and well, but obviously that changes from day to day. I also live on a farm which is two miles from the nearest village, which is only small anyway. I can tend to feel a bit cut off from life, and certainly hadn't met anybody before with MS, so knew nothing about it. The internet has been a bit of a lifeline for me.

"I regularly go along to the chatrooms at Jooly's joint, a great MS community site, at **www.mswebpals.org**, where I have a good old natter with all my friends there. We are not a depressing group, far from it! We are a jolly bunch of people drawn together, through a shared illness. We talk about anything and everything, and I am often in fits of laughter. I am such a positive person, and I find this is boosted by so many of the people that I chat to online. I have even been to meet some of the people I speak to, which has been great, and so uplifting.

"I've also been able to use the net to find out more about my illness. At first I used the search engines, and just typed in MS, and it came back with hundreds of sites. I found a lot of useful information, which was brilliant. I didn't have an on-call neurologist, but I could still find out all the stuff I needed at the touch of a button, without pestering my doctor's 24 hours a day! I definitely feel more in control of my life, as I can discuss things with online friends if I feel worried, and I can also find out information which I take along to my GP, and discuss with him. I feel like I am getting the newest information about everything, and I've been empowered to act on it."

Hot Tips – Chatting online

* Know your netiquette: avoid caps (SHOUTING), be polite, and check your spelling!
* Keep your messages short and clear
* Learn some abbreviations, like BTW (by the way)
* Use names so people know when you are talking to them
* Try out some emoticons to liven up your message, or to indicate when you're making a joke :-)
* Do not encourage offensive behaviour, or behave badly yourself
* Protect yourself. Read the chapter on Surfing Safely and be aware of risks when posting messages

Acronyms

Acronyms are a fun and fast way to express yourself when you're chatting online. There are hundreds of acronyms, the most popular are listed below:

LOL – laughing out loud

IM(H)O – in my (humble) opinion

BFN or **B4N** – bye for now

POV – point of view

ROTFL – rolling on the floor laughing

TIA – thanks in advance

TTYL – talk to you later

GR8 – great

CYA – see ya

Log on to **www.acronymfinder.com** to learn more, and prove you're a real chat pro!

Usenet newsgroups

If you can't find a chatroom to meet your needs then try one of the thousands of newsgroups. There are over 100,000 groups online, discussing every possible subject you could think of. The system is completely unregulated – a shining example of how the internet enables free speech in all its forms.

Usenet is quite simple. Users post a message or a question on the appropriate group and other people in the group reply – either via direct e-mail or the noticeboard. **www.newsreaders.com** has the answers to all your Usenet questions, and tips and FAQ's for configuring a Usenet account. However, the best way to start with Usenet, is to access it through **www.deja.com**, which has the most straightforward Usenet interface on the net.

To find a group that's right for you, you can either search via keywords, or browse the hundreds of categories available. The biggest clue to a group's topic is its name, which is usually quite self-explanatory. For example, there is a group called soc.feminism, which has any number of discussion threads relating to feminism. The most popular categories include:

alt.	alternative
misc.	miscellaneous
rec.	hobbies and recreation
uk.	UK issues
soc.	social discussions
biz.	business

If you use Usenet, you will have to make your e-mail address public to other users, this is a well-known source of Spam (junk e-mail). If you want to avoid it, give out a secondary e-mail address or use a non-existent address.

Communicating on the internet is fast, cheap, interactive and interesting. It can add a whole new dimension to your home, social or business life. Once you master the basic rules and systems and get used to the etiquette, there's a whole new world out there, from exciting new people to fascinating new perspectives and ideas. You'll get a warm welcome wherever you go so get out there!

You know it's time to log on when:

- You've run out of things to say to your friends
- You want to chat on a specialist subject
- You want to meet new people all over the world

Networking sites

Chat sites

http://chat.yahoo.com have hundreds of US and UK chatrooms, and also scheduled events, such as live celebrity chats online.

http://chat.excite.com has mostly US chatrooms, and you can create avatars to represent you.

http://msn.co.uk is now one of the UK's largest chat networks, with something for everyone.

www.thepark.com is a worldwide chat community created to promote world peace and international understanding.

www.worlds.net lets you play role-playing chat games in themed worlds.

www.hyperchat.co.uk has free public and private chat rooms for adults.

www.beefnut.com provides the perfect forum to let off steam! Complain about absolutely anything, or read others' complaints.

www.theglobe.com is a wide-ranging 'e-mail club'.

Women's networking groups

www.busygirl.co.uk has small monthly events for businesswomen.

www.hightech-women.com is a group for women working in technology.

www.womens-institute.org.uk is the homepage of the Women's Institute, an organisation which brings women together in local communities.

www.advancingwomen.com is an international networking and business site for women.

www.digital-women.com is a community site for women in business around the globe.

www.nwr.org is the site for the National Women's Register, an international organisation of women's discussion groups.

www.amazoncity.com/chat is a women-only chatsite from the US – chat in one of the permanent rooms, or create your own chatroom!

www.phoenix-network.org is a network of women working in new media and technology.

www.digitaleveuk.org is a group running women's events all over the UK.

www.e-womenforum.com helps women on the internet develop skills and meet up to exchange ideas.

www.flametree.co.uk is a network promoting the work/life balance.

Internet Relay Chat

www.mirc.co.uk is the UK home of Internet Relay chat, the biggest chat system on the net. This site explains everything you need to know to become an IRC user, in easy steps. It also has links to the main IRC chat channels and other help sites.

www.irchelp.org. Starting out with IRC can be tricky. If you get stuck, this website is your answer.

www.newircusers.com. If you're still finding your feet on IRC, log on here for some pointers.

www.ircnews.com for the latest happenings in the world of IRC.

http://mirc.stealth.net/mircrulz/ has all the netiquette tips for IRC.

Usenet

www.deja.com is your first stop on the net for everything newsgroup -related. It's the best and easiest net interface for accessing the newsgroups, with a complete list of groups. It will even walk you through the basics of using Usenet.

www.newsguy.com is another Usenet search engine for finding the newsgroup you're looking for.

www.supernews.com to get a personal Usenet account to download your favourite newsgroups and read offline.

www.newzbot.com is a simple directory of groups.

www.faqs.org. Each newsgroup has a list of rules and information about the group – these are all stored centrally on this site. Look up and read a group's FAQs before joining, so other members won't know you're a 'newbie'.

www.tile.net has comprehensive listings of Usenet newsgroups.

Chapter 8

Women at work

Forget the old boys club and join the new girls network! Welcome to the new economy, a world in which more of us are starting our own businesses, building careers and playing key roles inside and outside the home. A world that is connected, where work is becoming more open and flexible.

Just a few years ago, a harsh, aggressive attitude and a power suit were thought to be the two vital attributes women needed to win respect at the office. Today, however, ability is the essential credential, as proven by a new generation of female e-entrepreneurs, including Carole Dukes of ThinkNatural, Julie Meyer of First Tuesday and Cyber Group's Eva Pascoe. The success and fulfilment of women is happening across technology and industry; progress is just a little slower then we would like!

The internet has helped fuel a new, faster economy. Businesses now appreciate that the net not only represents a new channel for commerce and communication, but also can help to generate revenue through e-commerce and improved customer support. Companies are increasingly using the internet for more than just e-mail or research, but are managing their business processes, buying and selling, cutting overheads, and improving productivity. The internet has created a new generation of fundamentally different business models; intranets connect departments, and suppliers and customers are seamlessly connected via the net.

Web Life – Web-centric business

- Flatter hierarchies and more flexibility
- Increasing service-based focus
- Constant change is a way of life
- Speed and responsiveness are key
- The customer comes first

Opportunities of the new economy

What's more, companies who embrace the internet and look beyond the old rules are changing the way they manage people. They are hiring new types of employees, retraining staff, introducing flexible rewards schemes and working policies. The change has also opened up a whole range of new job roles. The old hierarchical structures are being relaxed. As companies develop an employee base that is internet savvy they are looking to recruit people with a wider range of skills and profiles.

You might think that these new opportunities are for technical people, like programmers or web designers. Not so. The internet has created a whole range of new jobs, especially in customer-facing roles, many with greater responsibilities and decision-making powers than ever before. There is real demand, too, and great opportunities for women with initiative. Working in teams, communicating with people, being able to manage a number of projects at once are the skills needed. It is not about technical skills but adding value through broader management.

According to a survey by the Chartered Institute of Personnel and Development, 58% of businesses had difficulties filling vacancies. These unfilled vacancies have a disastrous effect on the economy. Productivity, profit and growth all suffer. As a result, employers are starting to adopt more diverse (and tempting) training and recruitment policies for women.

Tip

Believe in yourself and don't underestimate your abilities. Even if you take small steps forward, they will soon turn into big confident strides.

Case Study
Sue Holly-Rodway

Sue Holly-Rodway is one of Sun Microsystems's successful women account managers, and has managed a large, demanding portfolio of media accounts such as the FT, BBC, Press Association and Mirror Group Newspapers. "The internet is an incredibly democratic environment. I use it as a tool, as a place to go find information. It's empowering to be able to inform yourself, to educate yourself, in order to be able to do your job better, even shop, to make your life easier, I believe that it's a really emancipating technology.

"The issue is awareness and useage of the internet amongst women. I personally believe that it is very healthy for the IT industry, the Government and the education system to really encourage girls to think of it as not just a 'speccy, tecchie, geeky' type thing but something that can be of real practical help to their lives. I also believe that the internet has revolutionised the ability for women to enter the market as a small business since the net is an ideas-based place and there's no reason why women can't have ideas as well as men.

"If you take a look at the businesses out there that use IT or the internet to underpin their value proposition, you will find many are run by women and the reason for that is the internet – you don't need the old boy network, you don't need the traditional ways of entering the market. I think the internet has begun to revolutionise women's access to the business community and will continue to do so if they use it as a tool. I hope that it will reduce the barriers for women and eliminate gender as an issue in being able to deliver on jobs of all types. I really believe IT can be a fantastic tool and also an exciting industry. I just hope that more and more women come to realise that."

Women put technology to work

Women and the internet, together make a great team. Multi-tasking, communicating and project managing are the skills most in demand in the new, internet-enabled economy. Women listen, are intuitive, and we like to partner. E-business depends on creating alliances and trading networks, which play to women's strengths as teamworkers. Most importantly, we have the energy, the motivation and the ability to deal with the change that's so vital to success in this dynamic and competitive environment. No wonder so many women find new technologies exciting.

In fact, women have been taking their places at the top of the once male-dominated Information Technology industry. Take Nikki Beckett, the UK's highest paid businesswomen, according to the Sunday Times. Her software company, NSB Retail Systems, earned her £14 million in the past year so she is a classic role model. She joined IBM to do a summer job after A-levels and got hooked by new technology. She seized the opportunity to progress, and formed her own company in 1994, yet still manages to balance this with her life with her husband and two sons.

The technology industry has many successful women, but the balance of power is equalising more slowly than it should be. Worryingly, the Women's Unit at the Cabinet Office warns that the proportion of women working in Information Communications Technology has fallen in recent years from 29% to 24%.

Businesses recognise the importance of redressing this shortfall. For example, Rebecca George, IBM's Head of Human Resources, believes passionately that girls as young as five should be interested in IT. As she says: "We've found that if you haven't persuaded a girl by the age of 14 that IT is interesting, then you have probably lost her."

As a result, these businesses, including Microsoft, **www.microsoft.com**, IBM, **www.ibm.com,** and Sun Microsystems, **www.sun.co.uk**, are developing strategies to attract and keep women. They have created a range of programmes, like 'taster days', to give schoolgirls a one day introduction to courses and resources for women returning to work.

Great places to work

The recent Sunday Times survey of the UK's 50 best companies to work for illustrates the opportunities provided by the internet economy, since so many of these forward-thinking employers are in the technology sector. See below for a selection from the list, or go to **www.greatplacetowork.co.uk** for further information.

1	Cisco Systems	Internet products supplier
2	Microsoft	Software supplier
3	Capital One	Credit card issuer
4	Timpson	Shoe repairer
5	Asda	Supermarket chain
6	Intel	Microchip maker
7	Abbot Mead Vickers	Advertising agency
8	Bacardi Martini	Drinks supplier
9	Morgan Stanley	Investment bank
10	Pret A Manger	Sandwich outlet
11	Sun Microsystems	Computer maker
12	Bettys and Taylors	Coffee and tea supplier
13	Agilent Technologies	Electronics company
14	Wragge & Co	Law firm
15	Hewlett Packard	Computer company

Web Life

- Many companies are actively recruiting women so broaden your horizons
- Enjoy a portfolio career and spread your skills across more than one job
- Pay is increasingly linked to performance
- Entrepreneurship is on the rise
- Take on projects that build up a skills and knowledge base
- New government training initiatives can refresh your skills
- Learn when it suits you, with online training programmes
- Use the internet to find out about vacancies
- Prepare for that all-important interview with some online research on the company

Returning to work? Stop here first.

If the thought of returning to work fills you with dread that everyone else will be more confident, more internet-savvy and more switched-on than you, you are not alone. Whether you're just beginning your search or are ready to start your new job and need a boost to your self-esteem or knowledge, help is just a click away.

As a starting point it can really help to visit chatrooms to talk to other women returners, get some hints and tips, and gain insight into other people's experiences. Try **www.lifeoutlined.co.uk**. With just a few friendly contacts you can start to build an online support network that you can call on whenever you need it.

Once you know what sort of job would suit you, you can probably find out more about it, what skills and experience are required and the sort of employers you'd be working for, on the internet. You can even find relevant training programmes and courses – many free of charge – to get you started or fill any gaps in your CV. Try **www.learndirect.co.uk** to find more courses to boost your work skills.

But don't underestimate the many skills you already have, from time management to multi-tasking. Many companies are now recognising the value of life skills and also offer job shares and to give you the chance to plan your working hours around the other demands of your life.

Work rights

It's important to know your working rights, and there are a number of Government websites with all the resources and information you need to keep up-to-date. **www.dti.gov.uk/er** is the website of the Department of Trade and Industry's employment relations department. It has information on all your rights, along with updates on legislation and employment issues in the EC. Other useful Government sites are **www.womens-unit.gov.uk** from the Women's Unit at the Cabinet Office, and **www.dfee.gov.uk**, the Department for Education and Employment online.

Case Study
Sangita Shah

Sangita Shah has been a director of The Leading Edge Company, an affiliate of KPMG, since early 1999, following a number of years at Unilever as a business analyst. She's also represented on the boards of a number of web-based enterprises advising on business development and brand strategy. So, is business today dominated by gender? "No. Today it's more to do with passion and commitment. In the new economy more people understand the different skill sets women have, where they are able to manage teams more effectively. Women are also now more aware of the power of these new skills.

"With the dress down trend it's interesting how people translate that into being less aggressive with a more acceptable demeanour. Now, in old as well as new economy enterprises, you see people being more expressive about who they are and not conforming to artificial male/female precepts."

So, how has IT helped women? Has it contributed anything to the creation of a level playing field? Sangita believes it has: "It's played a great emancipation role in women's lives, just with simple things like e-mails. They have enabled women to initiate conversations without any of the old artificial barriers getting in the way. And things like PDAs and mobile phones play a fundamental role in women being able to realise their potential in business by enabling them to achieve professionalism in the way they organize their job, tackle projects and manage their teams."

The workplace is changing, and this new economy, with its flexible structures, is creating new opportunities. More fulfilling jobs have opened up for women as the balance of power shifts to an economy where talent and determination shine through. With the lowest level of unemployment since 1975 and skills shortages being felt at all levels, employers are beginning to recognise the need for adopting new styles of management. New roles in the high technology and service industries are boosting the advancement of women. As the UK's economy transforms from a manufacturing to a service economy, this trend is set to increase.

Companies like those in the Sunday Times 50 best companies to work for are paving the way. They understand the value of happy employees, and create a workplace that allows people to balance work and home life. Investment in training, incentives to return to work after maternity leave, flexible hours, childcare policies, and availability of homeworking are what sets these companies apart. These employers, like Cisco Systems, Microsoft, Capital One and Asda have the edge in attracting talent. More businesses are set to follow their example as they discover that creating attractive workplaces pays for itself by reducing staff turnover and increasing productivity.

The challenge is to ensure that women play a prominent role in the new economy as it develops. We need to promote those companies that are female-friendly and encourage women to use their talents to fill the skills gap. We should leverage the power of the internet to extend this positive progress at work. Online learning, networking, and thousands of new internet jobs, combined with the flexibility the online age brings means the future looks good for working women.

You know it's time to log on when:

- You want to use your IT skills to your advantage
- You need more information on your employment rights
- You want to rejoin the workforce

Working women's websites

Information sources

www.busygirl.co.uk is a business technology portal for women, with services, advice and a business directory for budding female entrepreneurs.

www.eoc.org.uk is the Equal Opportunity Commission's website, with all the information you need to make sure there is sexual equality in your workplace. Don't get trapped by that glass ceiling!

www.dti.gov.uk/er is the Department of Trade and Industry's excellent resource to find out everything relating to your employment rights.

www.the-bag-lady.co.uk is a comprehensive resource and library of information for female business-owners.

www.opportunitynow.org.uk is an alliance of UK employers committed to promoting female employment. This site has excellent coverage of all the issues involved in recruiting and retaining women.

www.womenback2work.co.uk is an online resource for women returning to work, with all the information you'll find useful if you're thinking of returning.

www.womenreturners.org.uk also has great information about going back to work.

www.parentsatwork.org.uk will help you find out about your rights as a working parent.

www.networkingmoms.com is a US internet resource for working mothers, if you're looking for inspiration and camaraderie from women in the same boat.

www.childcarelink.gov.uk lets you search for the different types of council-run childcare in your area. See the chapter on Parenting Online for more help on this.

http://womenswire.com/work/ has great tips and other work-related articles brought to you by **www.women.com**.

www.workingwoman.com is a collection of resources to help working women all over the world.

www.womens-unit.gov.uk is the Women's Unit of the Cabinet Office, focusing on women's roles in the workplace.

www.set4women.gov.uk promotes female employment in science, engineering and technology.

www.hse.gov.uk is the homepage of the Health & Safety Commission, focusing on safety in the workplace.

At-work resources for women

www.digital-women.com is an international online community for women in business around the world.

www.businessadviceonline.org has advice for anyone running their own small business.

www.businesslink.co.uk is a local advice centre for small businesses.

www.thebiz.co.uk is a massive business-to-business information resource with a searchable directory for everything you'll need at work, from office supplies to training and seminars.

www.smartbiz.com is the 'how-to' resource for business it's a tips site with handy hints on everything business-related.

www.clearlybusiness.com is a business community with links and advice for working women.

www.scottishbusinesswomen.com is an online business centre for women.

www.wellpark.com is an integrated women's business centre.

Business news online

www.fastcompany.com, from Fast Company magazine, is a US-based company directory dedicated to the new ways of doing business, with practical guides to 'fast', e-enabled working, and an international directory of 'fast' companies.

www.ft.com is the homepage of the Financial Times, with all the day's crucial business news.

www.silicon.com will send you personalised IT news daily via e-mail.

www.redherring.com is the must-read update for anyone involved in the technology and internet sector.

www.computerweekly.com is Computer Weekly magazine online.

www.cnbc.com and **www.cnnfn.com** are both great international business news sites.

www.economist.com is The Economist online.

www.bbc.co.uk/business provides business news from the BBC.

www.bloomberg.com is Bloomberg's online resource.

www.wsj.com is the Wall Street Journal published on the net.

www.business365.co.uk is a business portal.

www.wwork.com is an online business magazine for women.

www.telegraph.co.uk is the Daily Telegraph online, with great business pages.

www.sunday-times.co.uk has an excellent weekly business section.

www.thetimes.co.uk has The Times' business pages available on your screens every day.

Chapter 9

The Balancing Act

Remember Superwoman? The woman who had it all? Step beyond the cliché and the reality is that we have moved beyond the 80s and now realise the key to happiness lies in balance. But with two thirds of British families having two working parents, achieving equilibrium between work and home can be difficult. The UK not only has the longest working week in Europe, but everyone is under pressure to achieve more than ever before. We all have so much to do and so little time. Even the most outwardly confident woman has to make difficult choices.

However, the internet offers hope. With a wealth of resources and services it can help us change the way we work, give us more free time, more choices and more opportunities. With the internet at your fingertips, you can find imaginative new ways to live your life on your terms.

Web Life – Balancing your life

- Get a job with an employer who offers flexible and friendly work policies
- Use e-mail to manage your communication and stay in touch from anywhere on the net
- Use reminder sites to keep track of important dates and appointments for you at **www.lifeminders.com**
- Keep track of your friends and family with a shared online noticeboard at **www.efridge.com**
- Speed up your research and get your questions answered online at **www.ask.co.uk**
- Log on and get in touch with your employment rights at **www.dfee.gov.uk**
- When you feel lonely or blue head for a chatroom for like-minded views at **www.everywoman.com**
- Have a traffic–free shopping spree from your computer at **www.shopsmart.com**
- Find out about the best employers and job vacancies on the net at **www.stepstone.com**

Workplace balance

We all want to achieve a better work/life balance, and be fulfilled at home and at work. The big hope is that the internet will help knock away more of the barriers to contentment; opening up training, increasing availability of information, providing opportunities to work from home and feel more balanced. Instead of fitting family and friends around your job, try finding more flexible ways to work, so you can make enough time for both.

If you're not happy with your home/work/life balance, there is plenty you can do about it. As many newly enlightened employers as well as the Government are realising, everyone has a life outside work. **www.dfee.gov.uk/work-lifebalance** is the Government's own site on the subject.

With the demise of the traditional nine-to-five lifestyle, companies are recognising the benefits of introducing a variety of new work-life policies. Asda, for example, is offering store management positions on a job share basis, while other companies are giving the option of shorter working weeks, part-time or term-time work. These choices have widened the opportunities in all types of jobs, for equal pay, benefits and career progression. Companies like Cisco Systems, **www.cisco.com**, Pret A Manger, **www.pret.com,** and Carphone Warehouse, **www.carphonewarehouse.com,** all offer female-friendly work benefits like flexible working.

You can use the internet to find out about the latest developments. Try logging onto **www.employersforwork-lifebalance.org.uk**. For more information about your employment possibilities, see the chapter on Women at Work, or check out **www.worklifeanswers.co.uk** with its easy to read advice on how to build a more balanced life.

Another option is to work from home, using the internet as your 'communications backbone', for e-mail, research or virtual meetings. See the chapter on Homeworking for more information.

Case Study
Helen Green

Married with two young children, Helen Green maintains a personal discipline that has her leaving the office late afternoon each day to ensure she's back in Woking to collect her children from the nursery. As an accountant in the London office of Saffery Champness, one of the UK's largest accountancy firms, it's not any easy choice to make. Not only does she have a full workload, there is also the risk that equally busy co-workers may not quite understand. But, as Helen says: "I'm only too prepared to take work home with me when it is necessary."

Like many professional women, Helen has a career and a family and has decided to balance the demands of her profession with the needs of her children. Is it an equitable life out there for career women? Answers Helen: "In accountancy it's still a male-oriented world although I think it's moving towards an equal mix of men and women. However, many women don't see it through as a profession. It's just too easy for women to give up, or go part-time and become a book keeper for a small business. Accountancy is quite a portable job, so you can work from home very easily."

And in such a male dominated world as accountancy is it intimidatory to be a woman? "Not a bit. There's no gender-based competition where I work, just the normal competitiveness between workers which you'd find in any company."

And what about balancing home, family and career? "It isn't a problem" states Helen: "You just apply a little common sense. Obviously if the children are sick then you have to take time off but you make it up later by putting in an extra few hours or taking work home. Everyone I work with understands that and has no issue with it."

Case Study
Jill Rawlins
Head of Public Relations,
Somerfield Stores

Balancing between career and family for Jill Rawlins
got easier the day when, while working at BT, they
made her their guinea pig for a new 'teleworking'
initiative that the telco was planning to launch
nationally. It coincided with the birth of Ben, her first
child. With daughter Lucy following a year after Ben,
and husband John pursuing his professional photography business,
some hard decisions had to be taken. It was pragmatism versus emotion.

In the end, since Jill's income was a guaranteed sum each month, she
and John decided that his career was the more malleable and he would
be better placed to see the children off to nursery and subsequently
school but, as Jill says, she was very lucky.

"Not many women with husbands or partners who also hold down
intense, taxing careers find themselves in such a position. I was lucky
because I was married to someone who was prepared to look at the
logicality of income and the flexibility of work.

"It's a great illusion that women can juggle career, family and stuff
a mushroom. When children are small and they sleep a proportion
of the day perhaps you can. But you still have to have efficient
childcare and that is where women are still trying to do too much
with the assumption that it can be done. It cannot. We are still not
in an equal situation today when it comes to the decision-making
on who's going to look after the children.

"Business is still dominated by men and they are still not universally
in tune with women who have careers and families. Women are not so
obviously disadvantaged as they were a decade ago but they still have
to put extra effort in today to ensure they don't lose out on any aspect
of their careers."

Changing life patterns is a challenge. Many people have felt trapped or feel held back by the knowledge gap and lack of information on their rights. Now the internet provides everyone with access to information on his or her rights and local opportunities.

The best place to start researching is probably the Government's own website on working rights at **www.dti.gov.uk/employment**. Anyone, from anywhere, can access information and start to feel more empowered and confident in their lives.

Networking, mentoring, feedback, emotional and career support are just the start of what help is available online. Nearly all the women's portals have chatrooms – you know it helps to talk. This is a new way to network, accessible to all women. So rather than trying to take on more and more or suffering silently with self doubt or stress – use the internet to help you find yourself, to find coaching, support and advice from other women.

We all have so much to do and that's where the internet comes in, from keeping in touch with friends to working from home – the internet has introduced new ways to get things done.

You know it's time to log on when:

- You can't find enough time in your day and everything's suffering
- Your stressful job is affecting the rest of your life
- You have so much clutter you can't find anything

Sites to balance your life

Useful online resources

www.flametree.co.uk will help you plan your time constructively and achieve that elusive balance between home and work. It also has links to life-coaching resources, if you need that extra push to get going.

www.lifeminders.com will e-mail you with birthday reminders, as well as newsletters and updates on a range of useful subjects. If all the information you need is already in your inbox, you'll free up the time you spend searching the internet for it!

www.en-parent.com is a US site for busy parents looking for help with the work/life balance. Useful information will get you heading in the right direction.

www.jugglezine.com is a great bi-weekly webzine from the US about balancing work and life, with fun articles on such subjects as 'making small talk' and 'dismantling the glass ceiling'. A fun and fresh approach to everyone's busy life!

www.worklifebalance.co.uk, **www.worklifeforum.com**, and **www.new-ways.co.uk** are more sites addressing the important issue of work/life balance.

www.efridge.com lets you create a virtual noticeboard and calendar which your friends, family and colleagues can access, so they can keep up with you from anywhere on the internet, for free!

www.ivillage.co.uk/workcareer is a huge UK resource covering all the info you need on balancing your commitments, with hot topics on everything to do with your career, as well as a multitude of other channels for women.

www.everywoman.co.uk is full of impartial info and lively chatrooms offering support and help from other busy women.

www.self-growth.com you'll find a comprehensive collection of articles and links relating to personal growth, self-improvement and self-help, covering all aspects of spiritual, mental and physical well being.

www.e-mum.com is the perfect site for UK working mothers, with articles, forums and a directory to help you find out about issues like childcare, homeworking and pregnancy.

www.ebedo.com has coaching resources, both in groups and on an individual basis.

Chapter 10

Homeworking

The internet has transformed the way we live and work. Thanks to e-mail, we can stay in touch with work colleagues at the click of a mouse, wherever we are. Through the net, we can find information, products and services, 24 hours a day.

One of the internet's biggest contributions to our quality of working life is that it enables people to work from home. With little more than a PC and an internet connection, we can be as productive and effective away from the office as in it. In fact, a BT/MORI poll showed that teleworkers are more relaxed and happy than commuters are.

As a result, homeworking is becoming big business. Fed up with rush hour traffic, the stress of office politics, constant interruptions and distractions, people are increasingly choosing to work from home. In fact, over two million people already work from home and the Henley Centre predicts that by 2006 more than 30% of the UK workforce will be home-based. See **www.henleycentre.com** for more information.

Interestingly, it's not just self-employed people, such as consultants or architects, who are working from home today. More and more companies are giving employees flexibility in where they work, creating a new breed of teleworkers who may work from home for a few hours, a day, a week, or full time. For the full story, log on to **www.youcanworkfromanywhere.com** to see how much easier your life could be!

Web Life – Homeworking

* Check out homeworking sites to find useful hints and tips to get you started at **www.ibiztips.com**
* Share real life experiences with homeworkers in online discussion forums
* Find work online, through contacts, through project bid and recruitment sites like **www.cyberworkers.net**
* Get linked into the range of affiliate programmes, details at **www.tca.org.uk**
* Learn about all the technologies you'll need at **www.telecommuting.org**

Making your homework easier

As well as connecting you to your colleagues and customers, the internet can provide all sorts of information, advice and services to make your homeworking life easier. Have a look at **www.homeworking.com** for advice, shared experiences and links to other useful websites.

The internet is also a great way to get work. Try **www.smarterwork.com**, a site where you can bid for a range of work projects. You can vary your rates depending on the project, how busy you are and how much you want the work. Distributed working, in which individuals or teams of people collaborate on project and contract-based work, is another phenomenon fuelled by the rise of the internet. **www.everywoman.com** is one of the first UK sites to pilot this and had over 700 women register as volunteers to their distributed working project.

If you're keen to go e-lancing (freelancing in the internet age), then take a look at **www.hightech-women.com.** This progressive women's networking group offers e-lance opportunities with a difference, including meeting and mentoring initiatives.

You're not alone

While many people relish the relative privacy of working from home, many feel a sense of isolation at being 'cut off' from the outside world. If you miss the camaraderie of the office environment, the internet can give you access to a wide variety of like-minded people. You can chat, exchange ideas and views; and ask questions at women-friendly portals such as **www.ivillage.co.uk**, **www.beme.com**, or **www.handbag.com**, or you can log on to sites specific to your life and interests to find new friends you already have something in common with. Find a group of e-friends at **http://uk.yahoo.clubs.com**.

Case Study
Katie May

"As the formulator for Yin Yang Beauty Care, at **www.yinyang.co.uk**, the internet has transformed my working life! I keep my technical records and references at home and I can receive all my emails at both our factory and at home. This means that I can work flexible hours – sometimes working in the evenings – writing leaflets and answering customer e-mails as they come in in the evenings and at weekends. It also means that I can e-mail documents to the office without driving to work and back, which is much better for the environment and saves a lot of time. I have been surprised that I can begin to handle this myself and can feel really involved in all the aspects of new products. The powerful laptop that I now use means that I can log on from the ISDN lines at home or local telephone communication systems anywhere I may go in the world. Not least of my internet pleasures is that I can write to my oldest friend in New Zealand and quickly send her photographs of the progress in my herb garden in Oxfordshire!

"Communication is very important in my business and to me the net has created a quiet revolution, I feel that it will just seep into everyone's daily routine as more and more people find it useful, with less time behind the wheel of a car, or on a train or bus and more time for both creative work and constructive relaxation. It is a stress-busting tool, one which we all need!"

Case Study
Elaine Yallop, Essex

"I work as a business consultant for energy and financial trading institutions translating their business requirements into system specifications. I recently had a baby and on returning to work joined a progressive consultancy company, Integra SP, who not only allow me to work part-time, but where possible I work from home. I use the internet to exchange documents and applications instantly with colleagues via e-mail, access financial and energy related websites and carry out research – all without leaving my study."

"I must admit I have never used a chatroom. I use my PC constantly for work and to start using it to have conversations with strangers would be a bit of a busman's holiday for me.

"With the cost of accessing the internet decreasing, people will be less wary of utilising the services offered by the internet. I have my laptop connected to an additional telephone line in the house, and pay a flat rate to AOL, so I have unlimited access with no additional telephone charges.

"As for work life I feel that many employers still need to be dragged into the 21st century and allow employees to work from home where possible. Unfortunately, they think staff won't be as productive at home as they are in the office. But I suspect most people would be so grateful to skip the commute each morning that they will ensure their managers are pleased with their work. With the services provided by the internet improving all the time, if you have had a bad experience, put it behind you and log on again."

Hot Tips – Considering homework?

* Find out your employer's policy on homeworking
* Read the practical advice on all business and legal issues before you get started at **www.dti.gov.uk**
* Discipline and planning are essential
* Avoid trying to juggle full-time homework with childcare
* Make sure you have your own space to work in at home
* Ensure you have the fastest internet connection possible, on a second phone line
* Online homeworking scams and get rich quick schemes should be avoided
* Remember homework will still be hard work

You know it's time to log on when:

* You've been sitting in traffic for two hours just on the way in to work
* You want to control your own workflow

Homeworking sites

www.homeworking.com is a good starting-point for researching your homework options.

www.gohome.com is a US site focusing on issues relating to working from home, with useful tips and an archive of articles.

www.youcanworkfromanywhere.com is a comprehensive homeworking resource.

www.ibiztips.com has hints and tips for homeworkers.

www.cyberworkers.net lets you locate your own work and bid on projects.

www.smarterwork.com is a project-work based site to help you fill your own work schedules.

www.elance.com lets you freelance from your computer.

www.freedesk.com enables you to access powerful office software, file sharing programs and 50 free megabytes of storage space. You can access your office from anywhere with an internet connection.

www.faxwise.com Send and receive faxes as e-mails.

www.jfax.com and **www.zipfax.com** both offer a similar service.

www.gilgordon.com is a good reference point for homeworkers.

www.combo.com will help you to research office ergonomics and improve your health and productivity at work.

www.yac.com is a sophisticated system which ensures all your calls, voicemail and faxes are sent to one easily accessible number, so you'll never miss another important message.

www.tca.org.uk is a European organisation formed to promote teleworking.

www.swiftdesk.com is a desktop you can access from anywhere on the net and store files, access your bookmarks or build a time planner.

e-Services to help you through the day

Need help with
managing your
busy life? Let the
internet come to
your rescue. Whether
it's the little things you need help
with, like finding a phone number, or if you've
made a life-changing decision to start your own
business, you're sure to find the services you need
from the huge amount available on the net. Covering
everything from much needed market data for a
business plan to finding a plumber for that leak in
the bathroom, all you need is to know where to look.

Hot Tips – Essential services online

- Link up with the professional help and information you need, such as accountancy, law, tax advice, professional bodies and venture capitalists. Try **www.businesspages.com** to link to what you need

- Get news and business updates e-mailed to your desk daily, so you can keep a firm eye on market conditions with minimal effort. Try the newsletters at **www.ft.com**, **www.redherring.com** and **www.silicon.com**

- Start your own dot com business with online help writing business plans, finding office space and getting that crucial funding, at **www.clearlybusiness.com**

- Get rid of those draughty windows and leaky roof by finding a builder at **www.homepro.com**

- Shop around for the cheapest utility bills at **www.buy.co.uk**

- Become a DIY expert by logging on to **www.naturalhandyman.com**

Female entrepreneurs

Good news! Entrepreneurial spirits are running high, especially among women. More and more women are starting their own e-businesses, and those women already running internet companies expect their turnover to boom over the next 12 months, according to a study by PricewaterhouseCoopers. The future's looking good for dot com women, but they must remain aware of the challenges of e-business, overcoming issues like recruitment, customer retention and profitability.

Do not let the risks put you off, because with a little help from the net you can find out how to minimise the risk and maximise the rewards of running your own business. You can get a closer understanding of the attributes you will need to be a successful entrepreneur on

www.busygirl.co.uk. It gives practical real-life help on how to get going on that road to success, and attending one of their networking events is a great way to build up those personal contacts which mean so much in today's business environment. No one should think about starting their own business without at least considering how they could factor in the possibilities provided by the internet. As Glenda Stone, managing director of Busygirl says: "I believe dot com companies provide greater senior management opportunities for women because there is less hierarchy and more focus on speed of thought and the ability to deliver. It's not about women being better or worse dot com managers than men – it's a business case for diversity with the management team".

The net provides the perfect starting-point to develop a business idea. Use the net to get the company started, validating the idea with online research, and even determine the right strategy by getting some top level business advice. **www.seekingcapital.com** offers women equal opportunities to access capital and it aims to proactively increase the number of businesses owned by women, with a section dedicated to making this happen. **www.business-incubator.com** enables you to build your business on the leading internet technology for as little as £15,000 for six months, as backed by Sun Microsystems, Cisco Systems and Oracle.

Starting your own business is exciting, but it requires vision, determination and management integrity. The challenge is making the right decisions, hiring staff, doing the financials, and, most importantly, creating customer loyalty. Overcoming the many obstacles faced by new companies is a massive challenge. The net offers help, networking groups, expert advice, and the opportunity to draw on the real life experiences of those who are already successful.

Services on offer on the internet step far beyond business, with a new breed of sites aimed at taking some of the stress out of life's major chores like moving house and getting legal advice.

Case Study
Soraya Duncan

Soraya Duncan is the co-founder and joint Managing Director of
www.buyme100.com – a one year old business-to-business bargains
portal that hosts a range of 'exclusive' products in seven consumer
categories including computers & electronics, fashion, health & beauty
and travel.

"The business world is getting better for women. With more and more
females in important, influential jobs, we are able to work together.
I often find that women who are focused and want to be seriously
successful do not get diverted by competing with those women who
have already got senior jobs. Career prospects for women are already
a thousand times better than in the days when my business was in early
embryonic form, but it's still hard for busy women to devote enough
time to all their commitments."

Now divorced, Soraya has two children from her marriage but is
fortunate to enjoy an extended family who all understand Soraya's job
and are willing and able to look after the children when the occasion
needs. "I'm working flat out now so that I'm able to take time off later
– to enjoy life, see my children grow up and find time to write a novel
that's built around my experiences!"

Public Sector resources on the internet

The Government has been a big supporter of the UK's online
revolution, and there are great Government sites, in all areas of
the Public Sector. **www.open.gov.uk** is the Government's portal,
which should enable you to find all the information you need.
www.e-envoy.gov.uk is thehomepage of the e-envoy, an office
set up to encourage UK citizens and businesses to get online.
The site has regular updates on the latest e-Government initiatives.

The Government plans to have all public services available online by 2005 – you can already apply for a passport, fill out a tax return, keep up with the latest legislative developments and access online legal advice. **www.ukstate.com** is the website of the Stationery Office, which aims to provide as much access to Government and public information as possible. **www.consumer.gov.uk** is a Government site dedicated to consumer issues, with advice and education for individuals and businesses.

Moving house

Even before you step out of the door to go house hunting, you can check out what neighbourhoods suit your needs. **www.move.co.uk** will give you all the statistics you need, from council tax rates to school pass rates to local entertainment and transport links. On **www.upmystreet.com** you can investigate local schools and check out the crime rates, to make sure you have a complete picture of an area before you make any decisions you might regret. Similarly, **www.undermystreet.com** and **www.homecheck.co.uk** will help you find out about an area's environmental considerations such as subsidence and flood risk.

Then save on the shoe leather by finding a new house online, browsing through thousands of properties anywhere in the world – although the large sites promoting your local estate agents will probably be the most useful, like **www.propertyfinder.co.uk** which lists local estate agents. Once you have found your dream property then **www.pickfords.co.uk** can help you make the move, with advice on packing and useful checklists. Even more usefully, register with **www.ihavemoved.com** and the site will notify everyone, from your bank to the Passport Office, of your change of address – saving you hours of time-wasting phone calls.

Once you've moved in to your new home, you might need to work on some home improvements. Avoid the cowboy builders by logging on to web directories of reliable contractors. **www.homepro.com** lets you search a database of trade professionals, and even contact them through the site. **www.referenceline.com** publishes unedited handwritten references for everything from home improvement specialists to car mechanics. The site itself is neutral, and willpublish bad references as well as good ones, so you can trust the recommendations. **www.improveline.com** is a directory of local contractors and will contact them on your behalf.

If you're thinking about DIY, log on to get handy hints and step-by-step guides on everything DIY-related. **www.naturalhandyman.com** is a good site to start with: do enough homework before you start wallpapering or re-pointing, and the job will go much more smoothly!

Motoring through the net

The internet has some great services for drivers, everything from learning to drive to buying a car. Two great starting points for all things car-related on the web are **www.theaa.co.uk** and **www.rac.co.uk**, the homepages of the AA and the RAC, providing traffic information, insurance and new car reviews. Find out what the experts have to say about cars at **www.topgear.com** or **www.autoexchange.co.uk**, two car magazines available online.

Logging on should be your first stop if you're thinking of buying a car, since the plethora of car sites takes all the hassle out of shopping around for a good deal on your new wheels. You could start by logging on to a manufacturer's website to find out more about what they are offering. Try **www.ford.co.uk**, **www.honda.co.uk**, or if you're feeling aspirational, **www.bmw.co.uk**. Vauxhall, at **www.vauxhall.co.uk**, are one of the pioneers of internet car-buying, selling direct to consumers through the internet.

Many sites make the most of price differences between cars for sale in mainland Europe and cars over here, by importing cheaper cars and passing on the savings to you. Try **www.carbusters.com**, a consumer site aiming to help people trying to buy their cars from Europe. **www.oneswoop.com** will search hundreds of UK and European dealers for quoted prices on your chosen model.**www.jamjar.com** is the car-buying site from Direct Line, which will shop around for the best deal for you. **www.autohit.co.uk** will trawl through UK dealers to find you the best prices for your car. **www.autobyetel.co.uk** combines new and used cars for sale, providing catalogue information and car reviews. Even if you're buying a second-hand vehicle, check it out with **www.equifax.co.uk**, who will cross-reference the car registration to make sure it's not stolen.

Legal assistance online

Everyone needs help from time to time with legal issues like making a will or moving house. There are plenty of sites which can keep you informed of your legal rights, or help you cut through red tape quickly and cheaply. **www.desktoplawyer.net** is a law portal which will help you compile your own legal documents for a small charge. They have a huge range of documents available, from simple divorces to wills. **www.lawrights.co.uk** has a wide range of information on your legal rights and you can download documents. **www.uklegal.com** is a UK directory of links to all areas of the Law. The net has opened up the world of law so that anyone can get online and find out about it. There's no need to rely on old-fashioned and expensive solicitors when you can be proactive on the internet!

Classified advertising

Whether you're looking to buy or sell, the classified ad section has always been a good place to look. Now the benefits of the internet are being put to good use, and classifieds are flourishing online. **www.loot.com** lets you place ads for free, and you can also search their database of ads for what you're looking for. **www.exchangeandmart.co.uk** is one of the best sources of second-hand cars.

Phone directories

There's no need to hunt through huge heavy phone books and the Yellow Pages any more – it's all available online, making your search so much quicker and more efficient! Find any UK phone number at **www.192.com** and **www.bt.com/phonenetuk,** whether it's a business or a person you're trying to track down. Search the Yellow Pages by business name or type, and area, at **www.yell.com** or try the Thomson directory at **www.thomweb.co.uk**. another popular online directory combined with a useful people finder is **www.scoot.co.uk**, **www.phonenumbers.net** is an international directory of phone numbers, addresses and e-mail addresses for businesses and individuals – search by country or continent. There's even a UK reverse phone directory at **www.warwick.ac.uk/cgi-bin-phones/nng**. **www.royalmail.com** will help you find an address or a postcode, and even let you calculate postal rates online!

So ease your workload and let the internet take some of the hassle out of major events. Whether you're finding a new flat or renovating your house with a bit of DIY, there is plenty of advice on every conceivable subject. Use the net to get some all-important professional advice, or to track down some vital information you might need to chase the next big business deal. The net is at your service, so make the most of it!

You know it's time to log on when:

- You're restless and need help making a move
- You want the latest news delivered to your desk
- You want to jump start your career and go it alone
- You're buying a car and don't want to be patronised by the salesmen

e-Services

Business service sites

www.businesspages.com is a business portal with links to everything business-related.
www.clearlybusiness.com will help you every step of the way when you're starting your own business.
www.ft.com helps you get share prices, search the global archive of business data and register for your own personal e-mail news service.
www.wsj.com is the Wall Street Journal online, crucial reading for budding entrepreneurs.
www.redherring.com
www.silicon.com
www.revolution.haynet.com
www.wired.com
www.economist.com
www.seekingcapital.com is a venture capital site.
www.business-incubator.com
www.companieshouse.gov.uk will let you research any public company in the UK.

Government sites

www.open.gov.uk is the portal to all Public Sector sites.
www.e-envoy.gov.uk is the home of the e-envoy.
www.inlandrevenue.gov.uk
www.pro.gov.uk is the Public Records Office online.
www.ukstate.com for the Stationery Office.
www.consumer.gov.uk for all consumer issues.

House and home sites

www.move.co.uk for all the information you need before you move house.

www.upmystreet.com to find out about the local area.

www.undermystreet.com for local environmental information.

www.homecheck.co.uk to check for subsidence and flood risk.

www.pickfords.co.uk has a great moving house checklist and other moving advice.

www.smove.com has everything to help you move house easily.

www.ihavemoved.co.uk will update everyone of your new address details on your behalf.

www.goodmigrations.co.uk has a move planner to help you.

Estate agents on the net

www.winkworths.com

www.foxtons.co.uk

www.underoneroof.com has over 50,000 properties to buy or let.

www.assertahome.com

www.propertyweb.com

www.londonhome.net specialises in facilitating private property sales.

www.easier.co.uk

www.houseweb.com

www.mooov.com

www.08004homes.com

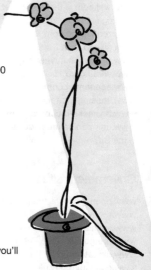

Home improvement sites

www.improveline.com has all the help you'll need in tackling your DIY jobs.

www.naturalhandyman.com

www.homepro.com to avoid the cowboy builders.

www.referenceline.com takes the guesswork out of hiring a contractor.

www.diy.co.uk is run by B&Q.
www.diyfixit.co.uk
www.diymate.com
www.diy.com
www.homebase.co.uk lets you buys essential DIY supplies from the net.

Motoring sites

www.theaa.co.uk is the homepage of the Automobile Association.
www.rac.co.uk for the RAC.
www.carbusters.com is a consumer car-buying site.
www.autohit.co.uk to shop around for a new or used car.
www.autobyetel.co.uk
www.oneswoop.com
www.autotrader.co.uk will help you sell your car, with classified ads
both on- and off-line.
www.jamjar.com is a new-car buying site.
www.new-car-net.co.uk
www.virgincars.com for new car bargains from Europe.
www.budget.co.uk, **www.avis.co.uk** and **www.thrifty.co.uk** will all help
you rent a car from the net.
www.dvla.gov.uk is the home of the Driver and Vehicle
Licensing Agency.
www.dsa.gov.uk is the Driving Standards Agency.
www.cyberdrive.co.uk will help you practise for your driving test for a
small fee.
www.driving.co.uk is the home of the BSM.
www.carquote.co.uk will search for a car insurance deal on your behalf.
www.equifax.co.uk is essential if you want to buy a legal used car.

Legal sites

www.legal-aid.gov.uk will give you help with legal aid.
www.wills-online.co.uk is an easy way to get your will done
– just fill it out on the net and for a small fee, this site will validate it!
www.wills-by-web.co.uk
www.makeyourwill.co.uk
www.divorce-online.co.uk will help you get a simple divorce quickly,
easily and cheaply.
www.landlord-law.co.uk has information about all tenancy issues.
www.desktoplawyer.net is a law helpdesk.
www.lawrights.co.uk will help you know your legal rights.
www.uklegal.com is a UK directory of law links.

Phone directories

www.192.com is Directory Enquiries online.
www.bt.com/phonenetuk
www.yell.com is the Yellow Pages online.
www.thomweb.co.uk is the Thomson Directory online.
www.scoot.co.uk has local information for wherever
you are in the UK.
www.phonenumbers.net for when the number
you're looking for is outside the UK.
www.royalmail.com for help with anything postal.

Chapter 12

Get A Job

Whether you're looking for a job or you're just browsing the opportunities around, you can find everything you need on the internet. From vacancies to training courses, to advice on preparing your CV and researching your prospective employers, you'll find a world of inspiration and opportunities online.

The advantages of job hunting on the internet are obvious. The net is huge, and there are literally millions of vacancies, all over the world, which you can access with one click of the mouse. Usefully, apart from jobs, you'll also find practical help and information to support and guide you. You can send your CV to hundreds of contacts instantly and simultaneously. You can job hunt from your desk, so it's quicker, easier and more convenient to find your perfect job.

Internet recruitment is also popular with companies – the Chartered Institute of Personnel and Development confirms that over half of all employers use the internet to recruit staff.

What are you looking for?

The first step is to decide what type of job you want. Do you, for example, want to try something new, do part-time work or develop your career? Start by visiting sites like **www.careers-gateway.co.uk** or **www.monster.co.uk** to see what kind and range of opportunities are available. If you think you'll need training, but need to find out more, check out **www.trainingzone.com**, a practical site with courses, directories and life coaches.

Prepare your CV

Most of the recruitment sites offer services which give you practical advice and help on how to create a CV, some giving you templates that you just fill in. At **www.monster.co.uk** you can even store five outline CVs so you can tailor your CV to the job you are applying for. You can create and store your CV online, together with covering letters. And if you're still not happy with your CV there are web sites that will create them for you, like **www.aperfectcv.co.uk** from £40.

Register with a job site

When you are happy with your CV you can register it with a recruitment site. One of the main services they offer is circulating CVs around talent hungry employers. On **www.jobsite.com** your CV is put on its own web page and then distributed to companies that might have jobs to match your skills.

Web Life – Making the internet work for you

- Take the initiative. Stop putting it off, go online and find out about new job opportunities

- Get help, valuable advice and support online to help you make the right career choices

- Create a CV with the help of some expert advice and templates online

- Jobs by e-mail. Make sure you find out about the latest job vacancies by signing up for the e-mail bulletins offered on many leading sites, such as **www.fish4jobs.co.uk**

- Do a self assessment. Many sites offer online questionnaires that help you find out what types of work you are best suited for. **www.topjobs.co.uk** offers a great careers survey assessment by analysing your likes and skills

- Work on your skills. Try online training to build your skills and confidence

- Promote yourself. Be positive about your skills and promote them actively by posting your CV on all the relevant sites

- Do some research. Get information about companies, training, types of jobs

- Register your wishes. Enter your ideal vacancy into sites like **www.totaljobs.com** so that you are the first to know when they get a job that suits you

- Smile! Embarking on a new start in life should be fun, check out **www.i-resign.com** to discover the best ways to resign

There is a whole range of specialist and general recruitment sites, aimed at all types of people. One with over 40,000 jobs is **www.reed.co.uk** which covers all key job sectors and offers useful learning tutorials. Then there are more specialist sites for graduates, travellers and volunteers looking for work with a worthwhile cause. Sign up with the one that best maps on to your aspirations. You can continue to find other sites to work with.

It is ironic that, although most of the recruitment sites offer CV services, many employers will also ask you to fill in an online application form rather than forwarding your existing CV. You have to register with them and key your details into an application form in their chosen format. This ensures that all applications are consistent and makes processing the applicants a lot easier.

In fact sending a CV as an attachment is very rarely acceptable. The biggest reason being the risk of viruses being contained in attachments, a valid reason why many sites will just not accept CVs as attachments. Also if you send your CV as a attachment you risk it being in an incompatible format, meaning it can either not be read or when opened it looks a mess. The safest option is for you to save your CV as e-mail text. You can cut and paste it and use it either as part of an online application form or send it as an e-mail.

A word of warning

But beware, many sites will not tell you who they are sending your CV to, which can prove embarrassing if it lands in your boss's inbox. Check the policy of the recruitment sites and only place yours on sites such as **www.peoplebank.co.uk** that seek permission before distribution, or specify what type of employers you are prepared for your CV to be sent to. Another option is to keep some of the sensitive data on your CV confidential, although this may detract from your CV's impact and relevance.

Case Study
Philippa Sholl

"In the middle of last year, I decided I needed a change, so I resigned from my job at a management consulting company in Melbourne, Australia and spent the summer travelling through Europe, before coming to London to look for a permanent role.

"I saved a search with relevant keywords on the **www.monster.co.uk** site, and it automatically e-mailed me when new positions were posted that matched my background. One Monday lunchtime I happened to see a position that seemed a perfect fit for what I was looking for. I quickly emailed my CV and a covering note to the consultant at TMP who had posted the ad, Jo Cumper.

"Actually, by the time I got back from lunch 40 minutes later, I had received an e-mail from Jo asking me if I would be able to come in for an interview. I met with her the following morning, and was quite excited by what I heard about the position. She then set up an interview for me with her client on the Thursday evening.

"Amazingly, the whole process from first seeing the position advertised on the net to receiving a verbal offer from the company lasted from Monday lunchtime to Thursday evening, and I am sure that using the net to search and apply for positions makes things move much more rapidly than they would have a few years ago, when we used to actually send copies of our CVs through the post!"

117

You know it's time to log on when:

- You hate the thought of going to work on a Monday
- Your boss has fewer skills than you do
- You are about to get your graduation results and haven't fixed your future plans
- You're bored and fancy learning some new skills

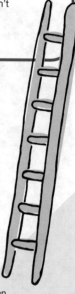

Job sites

Useful job hunting resources

Job hunting is the most popular pastime on the internet, and the vast choice of sites means finding your dream job is easier and faster than ever before. Click on to some of the options below to see what's out there for you!

www.monster.co.uk is the world's biggest recruitment site. This one-stop-shop is the perfect starting-point, packed with useful resources for the online job hunter. Register your CV, keep up-to-date via e-mail alerts, and scan UK and international job listings.

www.hotrecruit.co.uk has a wide range of casual and summer jobs all over the world for students and young people.

www.do-it.org.uk specialises in volunteering opportunities with UK charities.

www.topjobs.co.uk will send your dream job to you via e-mail, or even to your WAP phone, so you can keep in touch with the job market effortlessly!

www.workthing.com carries a wide range of employment information and links, with a large jobs database.

www.jobsite.co.uk is straightforward, award-winning site with both a quicksearch and a powersearch facility. Pin down the perfect job in seconds!

www.stepstone.co.uk is a pan-European jobs website specialising in the technology industry.

www.fish4jobs.co.uk has a huge jobs database, along with wide-ranging content including job news and recruiter profiles to help you narrow down your search quickly and easily. It's categorised by region so it's easier to find a local job.

www.peoplebank.com has personality tests for you to find out what kind of employment will suit you best. You can also start a career account, get interview tips and research the UK's leading employers.

www.jobsunlimited.co.uk has all The Guardian's jobs pages online, classified into broad sectors and searchable by keyword.

www.jobhunter.co.uk has a database of all regional newspapers' job listings, with over 21,000 individual jobs.

www.i-resign.com has the usual employment resources with a humourous touch.

www.agencycentral.co.uk and **www.rec.uk.com** will have detailed listings of expert recruitment agencies for your field, if you're in a specialised area.

Graduate recruitment

www.fledglings.net specialises in online student recruitment for graduate placement with employers nationwide.

www.gradunet.co.uk is a virtual careers office for graduates, with links to the top UK employers.

www.milkround.co.uk has opportunities for graduate job hunters with useful interactive tools.

www.gis-a-job.com concentrates on jobs in the IT industry.

www.totaljobs.com is the 'total careers site' with vacancies in all sectors.

www.alec.com focuses on giving you help on building your CV.

www.revolver.com is The Sunday Times' job pages online.

High street and temping agencies

www.adecco.co.uk is the online presence of the high street recruitment giant.

www.reed.co.uk has over 40,000 jobs.

www.brookstreet.co.uk will give you job listings and details of your local branch of Brook Street.

www.tempz.com is the first 100% online temping agency. You can hunt for your own assignments on their site, or build a homepage to make employers come looking for you!

Education Online

Whatever you need to learn, however you want to improve your knowledge, the internet is now integral to education, from playschool to university  **and beyond. Life is a learning experience after all, and however the internet can help, it's up to you to make the most of it.**

Thanks to the net, education is more flexible. You can learn in your own time and at your own convenience. You can do as much or as little as you want in a session. Many internet courses are available in a format which you can dip into whenever you like – or whenever you can spare the time. The flexibility of online learning is ideal for women's busy lives and has proved a big hit.

Another big advantage of learning online is the internet's interactivity – its amazing ability to make you part of a community wherever you are. You can chat online with other people on your course at students' forums, which may even be moderated by tutors, for extra help. There may also be bulletin boards where you can post questions, or search previous postings and reply chains to see what you can find that's relevant.

Finding a class that suits you has also been made much easier. You're no longer limited to your local area, or timetable. You can now even take courses from overseas. If you want to broaden your knowledge, you're in the right place.

Web Life – Learning online

- Distance learning opens up courses and home tuition to students all around the world. **www.open.ac.uk** has thousands of courses you can take from anywhere!

- Special educational sites can help those with learning difficulties, with information and guidance available for all special needs. Try **www.dyslexia-information.com**

- International students can find advice on courses and the cultural side of life abroad on **www.studyoverseas.com**

- Internet research will help you no matter what you're trying to learn. You can get a free interactive tutorial on **www.sosig.ac.uk**

- Surprise yourself by signing up for a new course on anything from line dancing to car repair. Find the course you want at **www.hotcourses.co.uk**

la pomme

The best way to find a course is through one of the educational websites with directories of courses. For example, **www.floodlight.co.uk** has an easy to use listing for all full-time and part-time classes in London. For university courses, try **www.ucas.ac.uk** where you can do a nationwide search for courses, universities, and even apply online.

But where the internet really comes into its own, in an academic context, is for researching information. Comprising a vast, global network of resources, the internet can tell you anything you need to know. So no more hunting through libraries, no more waiting for books: now you can find what you need in a few clicks. Try **www.academicinfo.net** and **www.ipl.org** to access a virtual library. Even if you don't know exactly what you are looking for, a quick search can turn up unexpected treasures, while serious students will benefit from the specialist online libraries.

If you want to enjoy the best of both worlds – community and flexibility, you can integrate the internet into your course. Even if there's no formal internet 'dimension' to your course, there's bound to be an internet discussion group or mailing list on the subject – no matter how obscure or specialised. Look them up at the search directories **www.liszt.com** and **www.deja.com.** Finding a group like this will give you added insight and a better perspective on a subject. You may also be able to chat online to other people on your course to share tips and advice, as well as meeting up in real life for classes. You might be able to e-mail your tutor for help and advice, too.

Case Study
Louise Havell, 22

"I use the internet all the time, for studying and also for fun! I'm a second-year student at Sussex University, studying American Literature. There are so many academic resources online, if I didn't use the internet I'd be missing out on a lot of useful information and research. My university has a big computer centre, so I can log on from one of the terminals at any time – no need to get my own computer! It's free as well, which is great.

"When I'm researching an essay, I generally start by searching on **www.google.com**, which is my favourite search engine. I like to set aside a bit of time when I'm researching, just to fish around the net for something interesting on a topic. It's worth spending the time to find out-of-the-way resources to make my essays as original as possible, so google's a great help because it's so comprehensive. I can also search my university's online archive of academic articles – some of them are available in full online, others are detailed in a catalogue. It means finding data to base my work on is so much quicker than physically hunting through dusty library stacks. There's no need to go on waiting lists for popular library books anymore either: the internet means an unlimited number of people can access the same information at the same time."

The Open University Online at **www.open.ac.uk**

The 200,000 students at the Open University, Britain's biggest higher education establishment, must be computer literate as a matter of course. Coursework, in all its forms, from short movies to documents, is supplied on CD-ROM disks. The University also offers interactive facilities, such as moderated conference forums, bulletin boards, and chatrooms. Students can also e-mail their tutor direct, send in their assignments electronically and enjoy exclusive access to the online library. This resource is particularly useful for the high proportion of foreign students who otherwise would have difficulty finding the resources needed.

Schoolkids online

Having pledged to get all schools online by 2002, the Government is well aware of the benefits the internet can bring to education (see **www.ukonline.gov.uk** for more about this). In fact, today's net-literate kids are using the internet to e-mail each other, get help with homework and look up their favourite subjects (invariably dinosaurs). One of kids' favourite sites is **www.ajkids.com**, a search engine geared especially for children.

Adult education

Adult education has, likewise, been transformed by the internet. No more weekly evening classes in draughty community halls, no more lack of choice or inconvenient timetables, you can learn whatever and whenever you want, wherever you are.

Web university

The internet has taken the university world by storm. Every student in full time education has his or her own e-mail address and can access the web for free. Even before you get to university, you can get help with the difficult process of choosing a course. Try **www.ucas.ac.uk** to start looking. Universities themselves are using the web and their own intranets (private websites) as central resources for educational materials such as course texts. It is often possible to access a university's library catalogues online, or even to book appointments with tutors on an online system.

The future

The educational world has always been ahead of the field when it comes to the internet. In fact, looking at how universities use the web is a good signpost to where the rest of the UK will be in a few years time. The potential is endless. Classes by video-conference? Virtual fieldtrips? Online exams? It's all possible. Prepare to learn something new – your way.

Tip

Online dictionary sites give you no excuse for limited vocabulary. Try **www.dictionary.com**, **www.thesaurus.com**, **www.onelook.com**, **www.yourdictionary.com**. Some are easier to use than others – experiment to find which one suits you best.

Case Study
Elaine Warmsley

"I access the internet every day. It not only helps me with the ongoing research I need to do as an NHS nurse, but helps me with my assignments, which I do as part of my vocational degree with the University of Central Lancashire. When I first started the course, I went to the library but it was far too time consuming. So I got my password and searched through the online journals for the information I needed.

"Thanks to the internet, I can look at other countries' health services, from their health policies to individual units. We are no longer isolated, but are part of the worldwide nursing community. I can save time, too. Accessing online research means that I no longer need to go into Preston, and spend 30 minutes looking for a parking space in order to use the University library there. Never again will I spend two or three hours searching, only to come out and find I've been clamped!

"I've been able to develop skills I've learned on the internet to improve systems at work. As part of my role I have set up a group of most of the critical care units in the North West of England to share best practice within our speciality of nursing. I have been amazed by the success of this innovation and I feel in order to communicate and promote the work of the group we need a web page, which is my next project!

"I feel the internet is already a part of many peoples' lives but they probably haven't experienced more than the minimum it can do for them. From personal experience, in our household the 'computer room' was the sole domain of the man of the house until I discovered the benefit it could bring to my life, and now it is very much a shared family resource."

Education sites

General educational sites

www.ipl.org is the Internet Public Library, a non-profit organisation with specific educational resources grouped for kids, teens and adults.
www.academic.info.net is a one-stop reference directory on all subjects.
www.bartelby.com has online access to a wide range of academic and reference texts, so it's extremely useful for quick research or if you're looking for quotations.
www.ehow.com is a massive site detailing over 15,000 step-by-step practical instructions on how to do anything from change a tyre to train your puppy. Or try **www.how2.com**.
www.askme.com enables you to pose a question on any subject to be answered by one of their experts.
www.libraryspot.com is a useful portal for all your reference needs.
www.learnfree.com offers video tutorials on hundreds of subjects.

www.boxmind.com is one of the largest academic resource directories, with 120,000 links across 30 subject areas.

www.tes.co.uk is the online version of the Times Educational Supplement, with all the education news, teaching vacancies and even online staffrooms to chat in.

Government education sites

www.dfee.gov.uk is the homepage of the Department of Education and Employment with information on all aspects of education, including the National Curriculum.

www.lifelonglearning.co.uk is a site to promote adult learning, detailing all government initiatives to promote life long learning.

www.basic-skills.co.uk is the homepage of the basic skills agency, set up to help everyone strengthen their basic skills.

www.ngfl.gov.uk is the portal for the National Grid For Learning with a collection of education-oriented sites for all levels. Perfect as a jumping-off point if you're thinking about returning to learning.

www.qca.org.uk is the homepage of the Qualifications and Curriculum Authority to promote coherence in education.

www.worktrain.gov.uk is the National Jobs and Learning site, from the Department of Eduction and Employment.

Kids' education

www.eduweb.co.uk is an education website for teachers and pupils with a carefully-filtered directory of educational web pages and internet resources.

www.atschool.co.uk is a learning portal for primary school-aged kids, with good resources for parents too.

www.virtualschool.co.uk sends courses by e-mail in all the main subjects, plus interactive help with expert input.

www.edview.com is a great educational directory with kids' links, grouped into subject areas.

www.funschool.com is a US site with free online educational games for kids of all ages. **www.funbrain.com** is a similar site.

www.schoolzone.co.uk has 30,000 free resources for kids, compiled by UK teachers.

www.learningstore.co.uk is a comprehensive e-commerce site selling all kinds of educational and reference software, for kids and adult learning.

www.dyslexia-information.com caters for all sorts of special needs, concentrating on helping with reading and writing difficulties.

www.projectgcse.co.uk has some great tools to help you with your GCSE revision.

www.gcse.com has past papers and useful revision tips to help you do your best at exam time. Or try **www.revise.it**.

www.bbc.co.uk/education/gcsebitesize is a great study aid, running in conjunction with the BBC's bitesize TV revision programmes.

www.a-levels.co.uk has a great list of links for A Level students, organised into subject areas.

www.homeworkelephant.co.uk has interactive revision and homework help for all ages.

www.learn.co.uk is The Guardian's education site with in-depth information on the core subjects.

www.homeworkhigh.com is Channel 4's homework site, where you can e-mail real teachers with your questions.

University

www.student-world.co.uk is a portal for UK students, with fun content revolving around student life.

www.nus.org.uk is the homepage of the National Union of Students.

www.yoonee.com is a light-hearted look at student life. You can search for, buy and sell textbooks, find academic papers and look for a job.

www.studyoverseas.com is a good site for research if you want to learn abroad – search for foreign universities or find out about countries.

www.helpineedto.co.uk will teach you all the essential student lifestyle knowledge if you're living away from home for the first time.

www.student123.com has a range of resources for students, from academic help to finding a job.

www.bigbluespot.com is a student portal offering free PCs.

Adult education

www.learndirect.co.uk is a government-backed website offering you the chance to learn for fun or work, on computer-based courses that anyone can master. There are 1,000s of learning opportunities!

www.u3a.org.uk is the homepage of the University of the Third Age, a learning community for retired people, running courses throughout the UK.

www.open.ac.uk is the portal for a range of linked Open University websites. Log on to see the perfect educational website.

www-idcl.open.ac.uk is the homepage of the international arm of the Open University, with over 30,000 distance learning programmes from over 1000 educational institutions worldwide!

www.berlitz.com is the homepage of the famous Berlitz language schools – buy a course or join an online discussion.

www.linguaphone.com – buy a Linguaphone language course online.

Course finders

www.hotcourses.com is a huge, easy-to-use search directory for all university and college courses, with details of over 100,000 individual courses.

www.floodlight.co.uk is London's best guide to part-time and full-time courses, with details of every course and college in London. From accounting to yoga.

Chapter 14

Shopping Guide

Whether you want to do some serious damage to your credit card or just do a bit of window shopping, it's time to head for your browser, not your local high street. While British men tend to buy expensive goods on the internet with the same time saving mentality they tend to have when in the high street, women tend to make lower value purchases online and do a lot more browsing.

Men and women still view online shopping differently, women use the net as a way to look up prices before they buy, but still love the traditional shopping experience. The trend is all set for more women to spend more time online doing internet shopping, it's a great use of your lunch hour and frees up the weekends.

Case Study
Vanessa Lowe

"For those with kids, or mobility problems, the internet is a great way to shop without having to cope with transport and dragging around the pushchair. UK surfers can find everything online, from the weekly groceries, to kids toys to designer clothes. Many mainstream retailers have set up online and provide the wide variety of items they do in shops.

"If I were to tell you I buy myself two extra hours a week for a fiver…you might say I sound a bit mad. Looking after a baby, a husband, working part-time and re-furbishing an old house can send you a bit crazy, but being able to save time by shopping online has helped keep me sane!

"I used to drive 30 minutes to my nearest supermarket, lug round a trolley for an hour and struggle back weighted down with bags and a screaming baby for another half an hour. End result, two hours of regular tedium that risked ruining my Fridays forever. That was until I started shopping online. Now, I simply click onto to **www.iceland.co.uk**, order what I want in minutes and let someone else select it, pack it and carry it all straight to my door. Believe me, it really is that easy and once you've been shopping online a few times, you'll be saving and re-saving lists, according to different occasions; weekly shops, dinner parties, barbecues or even accessing recipes where the ingredients are automatically downloaded to your virtual shopping trolley. And all this will cost you no more than your net time and the regular £5 delivery charge. Bargain I say, especially when it stops all those unnecessary impulse buys!

"Being superwoman isn't about working harder, it's about working smarter and online shopping is definitely the way ahead. I haven't found an online site to sort out the washing, cleaning and ironing yet… but I'm still surfing in hope!"

Top 5 types of Products Purchased Online by UK Women*

(33%)   (23%)   (18%)   (13%)   (7%)

Books   Music   Holiday/   Clothes   Electrical
         CDs   Travel   Goods
                  Related

*Source: NOP "Women on the Web" January 2001

Food for thought

Keeping the fridge stocked is a constant battle, having to dash to the shops only to end up in an hour-long queue at the checkout. So why not order online and get your groceries delivered to your door in a matter of hours? Although Forrester Research suggests that much less than 1% of food is bought online it is set to increase with the major investments in online delivery by the big supermarkets.

www.tescodirect.com is leading the way offering an online service from more than 300 stores and over 40,000 items to choose from – giving coverage to most postal areas in the UK. **www.iceland.co.uk** also has 95% coverage of the UK by offering delivery from all its local stores. Although it may take a while to place the first order when you have to enter all the registration details, it gets easier the second time as you amend your shopping basket needs.

Even if you do not fancy buying your perishables like meat and vegetables online, ask yourself why it makes sense to come home with heavy bags of pet food or washing powder when you could have had them delivered to your door. And at most of the big stores like **www.sainsburys.co.uk** and **www.waitrose.com** you can usually stick with your favourite brands. Add a little spice and flavour to your shopping basket by visiting one of the many niche services online that will help fill the cupboards with produce that is harder to find, like quality organic food. **www.organicsdirect.co.uk** delivers fresh fruit, vegetables, breads, baby foods and much more. And if you are preparing for a party why not sort out all the catering needs online, see the *Celebrations* chapter.

Auctions

Liven up your internet shopping experience by taking part in an online auction at sites like **www.qxl.co.uk**, **www.ebay.co.uk**, and **www.amazon.co.uk**. Many of the most popular auction sites give you the chance to bid for a whole range of new and used goods, everything from washing machines to Beanie Babies. The way it works is that you place a bid on an item for sale on the site, just like in a real-world auction. There is a time-limit for the auction, usually a few days, to allow everyone to put a bid on. If you are outbid, you can raise your bid – it's worth keeping an eye on how the auction is going – all the information will be listed on the site. If your bid is successful (or not) the site will let you know, and you'll receive the item in the post a few days later.

Auctions are a great way to shop on the net: they are perfect for picking up bargains, they are fun and addictive, and you're able to locate, and buy things you wouldn't normally find for sale, such as collectibles.

Case Study
Annabel Jermyn

"With five young kids all under seven – five-year old triplets, a three-and six-year old, the internet is a real helper, since it's impossible to drag them all around the shops! The first and most useful site is **www.tesco.co.uk**, which is fantastic – delivering your groceries within two days for a £5 delivery charge. The delivery used to take four days which meant far too much pre-planning of meals, now the wait is much better.

"Another life-saver is buying Christmas presents and gifts online, **www.thewhiteco.com** do some really nice baby gifts and gift wrap them for you. **www.letterbox.co.uk** are great for kids stocking-fillers, and with catalogue sites like these you often get an extra discount when ordering online.

"I do lots of browsing, in fact I'm an online shopaholic, getting as much pleasure from finding ideas online as I do in the shops. It's been great for home decoration tips, and I've got the kids some really good quality clothes from **www.boden.co.uk**, who also do adults' clothes. Although I have come unstuck a few times, like this Christmas when Woolworth's did not deliver the presents I'd ordered for my nieces and when I chased it up they couldn't find an order number but in the end they sorted it all out and compensated me for the hassle – now I order well in advance to avoid disappointing anyone.

"Finding bargains may be fun, but it's the time factor that's the big advantage, for those few hours the kids are at playgroup I can sort out the shopping without having to worry about parking and being late for the nursery school pickup."

Looking good

Buying clothes online is easier than you think, you have online access to a wide range of items including the latest designer gear. **www.designerdiscount.co.uk** has some offers that would be difficult to match down the local high street. **www.yoox.com** is a site offering the top designers at massive discount. And even if you do not know what fashions you want then where better to get some top fashion advice than the net? **www.confused.co.uk** gives you a guide to this season's cool gear. Or cut down your magazine bill by logging on to **www.vogue.co.uk** or **www.ellemag.com**.

Head for **www.zoom.co.uk** to find a great online shopping mall. With its easy to use directory you will find yourself shopping in some top brand stores like **www.principles.co.uk**, **www.tops.co.uk** and **www.burtonmenswear.co.uk** to name but a few.

www.freemans.com and **www.kaysnet.com,** the leading catalogue companies, offer a massive selection of goods at really good value – all backed with their excellent distribution and customer service networks.

Of course completing that outfit will require a few accessories, bags and shoes. **www.intofashion.com** offers a great service with free delivery in the UK. **www.jewellers.net** can also add those all important finishing touches with a huge selection of fashion jewellery.

Comparison shopping

One of the most useful internet shopping tools are the price comparison sites. Rather like search engines, they will look all over the net for you to find the cheapest prices – you just enter in the product you are looking for, and the site will do all the hard work for you. Shopping around for the best bargains has never been so easy! Try sites like **www.shopsmart.com** and **www.checkaprice.co.uk** to see how much you could be saving.

Hot Tips – Shopping safely

- Think brands. Opt for reputable, branded online stores

- Check out the delivery policy. Delivery times can vary from hours, to weeks and months: make sure it will arrive when you need it

- Compare prices. Try some of the buying clubs or visit one of the price comparison sites that show you where to go for the best bargains

- Be cautious. Never give away your credit card PIN number and only give your personal/credit card details when you are sure it is a secure site

- Use a credit card. By using your card for payment you will be covered with more credit protection; the exact details depend on your card

- Know the price. Make sure you know the total purchase price, including delivery costs before you complete the transaction

- Check out the returns policy. How many days have you got to return goods and who pays for postage?

- Damage limitation controls. Make sure you are not liable if goods are faulty on delivery

- Record the transactions. Always save copies or printouts of online orders, confirmation e-mails and delivery notes for future reference

- Check out customer support provided. The best sites are backed by phone support. If you have a problem, contact them immediately

- Know the size. Try to find a sizing guide on the site because sizes are not standardised

- Accuracy can vary. Remember that screen colours and textures may not be completely accurate

Web Life – A guide to spending online

- More net shoppers have bought a book online than anything else. The likes of **www.amazon.com** clearly started the shopping revolution, so check out huge number of book retailers like **www.waterstones.co.uk** or **www.bol.com** and find some great books and bargains

- Computer hardware and software are popular online buys, where you can get full lists of specifications of the products and some great prices at online stores like **www.comet.co.uk**, **www.dixons.com**, and **www.tempo.co.uk**. Or try an online electronics specialist like **www.jungle.com**

- Get your groceries online and beat the queues by letting the supermarket come to you at **www.tescodirect.com**, **www.sainsburys.co.uk**, **www.waitrose.com**

- From designer dresses to babygrows the internet is packed with clothes in every shape and size, for the best selection you are best head for one of the online shopping malls like **www.zoom.co.uk**

- Satisfy your sweet tooth with some Belgian chocolates or some candy from the vast selection of online sweeties. **www.thorntons.co.uk** will deliver your favourites, or try **www.chocexpress.com** which offers a huge selection and free delivery

- Build up your home video and DVD collection from the thousands of titles available online, often than at less than high street prices, **www.filmworld.co.uk**, **www.blackstar.co.uk**, **www.videoshop.co.uk**

- Music of every kind can be found online, from unsigned artists to the pop classics **www.cdnow.com** has a huge archive, as do the mainstream names like **www.amazon.co.uk** and **www.hmv.co.uk**

- For gadget girls the net offers the coolest mobiles and life accessories from heart rate monitors to Billy Bass, the singing fish. Try **www.gadgetshop.co.uk**, **www.carphonewarehouse.com**, and **www.virginmobile.com**

You know it's time to log on when:

- You've tried on everything in the high street
- You can't face another Saturday struggling round the supermarket
- You're looking for a hassle-free bargain

Shopping websites

Shopping directories and comparison sites

www.kelkoo.com
www.shopgenie.com
www.shopsmart.com
www.valuemad.com
www.excite.co.uk/shopping
www.freeserve.com/shopping
www.topoftheshops.co.uk
www.beenz.com
www.checkaprice.com
www.which.net
www.mytaxi.com
www.shopsafe.co.uk
www.obongo.com
www.ybag.com
www.shoppingunlimited.co.uk
www.priceoffers.co.uk

Internet malls

www.shoppingarcade.co.uk
www.ishop.co.uk
www.dolondon.com
www.indigosquare.com
www.uk.shopping.yahoo.com
www.zoom.co.uk

Books

www.amazon.co.uk – arguably the most famous e-commerce site on the net, this huge online bookshop also sells music, videos and computer games. Prices are generally cheaper than in bookshops, with many more books available. However, delivery charges might offset the price discount. You can even search for rare and second-hand books.

www.bol.co.uk is as large as Amazon, with similar range of content.

www.alphabetstreet.co.uk offers free delivery within the UK.

www.whsmithonline.co.uk is the online presence of the UK's best-known bookshop.

www.waterstones.co.uk the website of Waterstone's bookshop.

www.dillons.co.uk

www.stanfords.co.uk is the homepage of the world's finest map and travel bookshop.

www.audiobooks.co.uk buy your favourite books on tape.

www.murderone.co.uk is the site of a specialist crime and sci-fi bookshop.

www.zwemmer.co.uk specialises in books about art, architecture, design and photography.

www.bookshop.co.uk is a UK internet-only bookshop offering big discounts.

http://bookshop.blackwells.co.uk is the UK's biggest academic and professional bookseller online.

www.books.co.uk lets you compare prices of all the UK's online booksellers, and also has a directory of all bookshops online. **www.bookbrain.co.uk** will search 14 UK booksites for the cheapest price for your book.

Buying music online

Most of the online bookstores sell music as well, but it's also worth checking out the sites below.
www.cdnow.com – buy CDs, DVDs, Videos and games online. You can also listen to music samples and get the latest music updates.
www.cd-wow.com is one of the best sites for bargains, with a limited range of CDs for under £10.
www.clickmusic.co.uk is a vast music directory with an e-commerce section and links to major music retailers on the net.
www.cduniverse.com is another huge US music site.
www.towereurope.com is Tower Records' online presence.
www.hmv.co.uk everything you would expect from HMV, on the net.
www.blackstar.co.uk is the UK's best site for videos and DVDs.

Fashion online

www.fashionbot.com is an invaluable online fashion search directory.
www.burtonmenswear.co.uk
www.dorothyperkins.co.uk
www.evans.ltd.uk
www.frenchconnection.com
www.gap.com
www.gapkids.com
www.hm.com – Hennes and Mauritz online.
www.www.eu.levi.com – Levis jeans.
www.marks-and-spencer.co.uk
www.monsoon.co.uk

www.mossbros.co.uk
www.jojomamanbebe.co.uk – maternity and babyclothes.
www.mothercare.com
www.next.co.uk
www.principles.co.uk
www.redordead.co.uk
www.riverisland.com
www.thomaspink.co.uk
www.tie-rack.co.uk
www.topshop.co.uk

Catalogues

www.boden.co.uk – quality clothes for men, women and children.
www.freemans.co.uk – Freemans catalogue online.
www.grattan.co.uk
www.shoppersuniverse.com
www.hawkshead.com
www.redoute.co.uk – La Redoute online.
www.landsend.co.uk – the Lands End Catalogue on the net.
www.llbean.com – the L L Bean catalogue.
www.racinggreen.co.uk
www.kaysnet.com
www.argos.co.uk
www.indexshop.com
www.innovations.co.uk

Designer bargains

www.bestofbritish.com
www.luxlook.com
www.littleblackdress.co.uk
www.designerheaven.co.uk
www.yoox.com
www.intofashion.com

www.theclothestore.com
www.zercon.com
www.zoom.co.uk
www.designerdirect.co.uk
www.haburi.com
www.bluefly.com
www.designerdiscount.co.uk

Underwear online

www.splendour.com
www.figleaves.com
www.rigbyandpeller.co.uk
www.smartbras.com
www.knickerbox.co.uk
www.bravissimo.com
www.yzea.co.uk

Accessories and shoes

www.shoe-shop.com
www.accessorize.co.uk
www.claires.com
www.cooldiamonds.com

Cosmetics and health

www.boots.co.uk
www.superdrug.co.uk
www.uk.avon.com
www.thebodyshop.co.uk
www.perfuma.com
www.clinique.com
www.loreal.com
www.olay.com – Oil of Olay's site.

www.revlon.com
www.tisserand.com sells aromatherapy products.
www.nivea.co.uk
www.sephora.com
www.yinyang.co.uk sells naturally balanced beauty products.
www.bobbibrowncosmetics.com
www.gloss.com
www.crabtree-evelyn.co.uk
www.directcosmetics.com
www.perfumeshopping.com
www.lookfantastic.co.uk is the place to buy discounted designer hair products.
www.island-trading.com has discontinued cosmetics.

Department stores

www.allders.co.uk
www.argos.co.uk
www.bentalls.co.uk
www.bhs.co.uk
www.debenhams.co.uk
www.fortnumandmason.co.uk
www.harrods.com
www.houseoffraser.co.uk
www.indexshop.com
www.johnlewis.co.uk
www.liberty-of-london.com
www.marks-and-spencer.co.uk
www.selfridges.co.uk
www.woolworths.co.uk

Grocery shopping

www.asda.co.uk
www.budgens.co.uk
www.co-op.co.uk
www.iceland.co.uk
www.morrisons.plc.uk
www.organicsdirect.co.uk – get a wide range
of organic food delivered to your door.
www.purelyorganic.co.uk
www.bbr.co.uk – order your wine from Berry Bros. huge wine
cellar, with over 1,000 different wines to choose from.
www.safeway.co.uk
www.sainsburys.co.uk
www.somerfield.co.uk
www.tesco.com
www.waitrose.co.uk
www.thorntons.co.uk
www.leapingsalmon.com – instant meal kits delivered in one day.
www.lastorders.com – get any kind of alcohol delivered.
www.chateauonline.co.uk – French wines on the internet.
www.jackscaife.co.uk delivers traditional meats around the world.

Auctions and bargains

www.letsbuyit.com lets you join a buying club to bring a product's
price down.
www.bigsave.com
www.sothebys.co.uk and **www.christies.com** specialise in art
and antiques.
www.exchangeandmart.co.uk has classified listings, specialising
in second-hand cars.
www.qxl.co.uk
www.ebay.co.uk
www.amazon.co.uk has an expanding range of auctions.
www.ebid.co.uk

www.internetauctionlist.com is an auctions portal.
www.auctionwatch.com has listings of all internet auctions.
www.auctionguide.com is an auction sites directory.
www.fsauctions.co.uk

Gifts and flowers

www.flowersdirect.co.uk
www.interflora.co.uk
www.jane-packer.co.uk
www.teleflorist.co.uk
www.codygifts.com
www.thegadgetshop.com
www.needapresent.co.uk
www.hallmark.com
www.tiffany.com

www.giftdeliveryco.com – fun and unusual activity-based gifts.
www.giftstore.co.uk
www.giftinspiration.com
www.propagangsta.com – fun, young novelty gifts like
inflatable armchairs.
www.hugsandcuddles.co.uk specialising in teddy bears.
www.alt-gifts.co.uk sells alternative gifts in a wide price range.
www.boxedup.co.uk – stylish and unusual gifts.

Chapter 15

Money Matters

With its global connections and instant communications, the internet is ideal for all kinds of financial services and is already revolutionising the way we manage our money. From banking, to online financial advice, to playing the stock market, going online doesn't just mean spending money, but making the most of it too. Millions of people in the UK already do their banking online, so why don't you join them?

Are you sick of spending your lunch hour queuing in the bank? Do you want to invest in the stock market, but don't know where to start? You might want to start banking online and eliminate a lot of the hassle of managing your money.

A competitive, flexible, democratic environment, the internet has given us greater 'consumer power' than ever before. It gives us choice, flexibility and some great deals. Most people already appreciate that you can pay your bills at 2 am in your pyjamas. But fewer people realise that you also get excellent rates of interest on online accounts, because, with lower overheads, 'virtual' banks can pass on their savings to you.

Likewise, because changing to another online account is much simpler than with a traditional bank and, because all the information is in one place, it's easier to shop around for the best deals. Log on to **www.moneyextra.com** or **www.moneygator.com** for comparison tables for financial products. Financial websites are much quicker and more straightforward to use than they used to be, and there's plenty of help if you get stuck. You'll never need to queue up to shout through a glass window again!

Web Life

- Use the internet to access your accounts at any time, from anywhere
- Get your bank balance sent direct to your mobile phone at **www.cahoot.com**
- Go comparison shopping for financial products to get the best rate at **www.smartmoney.com**
- Pay your bills in a click from your bank's website
- Find out whatever you need to know at **www.thisismoney.co.uk**
- Be a financial insider, get tips online from those in the know at **www.citywire.co.uk**
- Enjoy the best rates with an online account from a virtual bank

High street banking on the net

If you're new to online finance, an ideal start (and one of the most popular forms of online banking) is to use the internet facilities of the bank you're already with. All the large high street banks and building societies now do this. For example, **www.lloydstsb.com**, **www.hsbc.com**, **www.barclays.com**, **www.natwest.com**. See below for full listings of all banks online. You won't have the hassle of changing accounts – your account numbers and existing payment arrangements will stay exactly the same. You can still bank as normal through your bank branch, and continue your relationship with your bank manager.

To get started, simply go to your bank's website and click on Personal Banking. It will have details on how to register, what you need and instructions on how to use the website. Generally, you should be able to register right away, with information such as your date of birth, account numbers and sort code or PIN number.

Once you've registered, you should be able to do everything you need to do from the comfort of your computer or even, to an extent, your mobile phone. You can, for example, check your balance and bank statements, transfer money, pay your bills, set up standing orders and direct debits, even download information into finance software such as Quicken and Microsoft Money. The bank will have customer service support staff on hand and you can e-mail them with your questions or any problems you're having. You will still be able to use all the services you would normally get from your bank branch, such as buying insurance, with the added convenience of an online connection.

Case Study
Sara Adamson

"I use the internet for all my banking, and I must say it's made everything so much easier! I'm not very good with money, so anything that takes the hassle out of managing it, can only be of benefit to someone like me! I can honestly say I've not stepped foot inside a bank for over a year, ever since I started banking online.

"I have a current account at **www.lloydstsb.com**, and a credit card with **www.egg.com**. Both were really easy to set up; I was already using Lloyd's telephone banking service, so registering for online banking was just a matter of typing in my membership number and a password, and doing a few easy set-up operations at the beginning. Egg was equally easy, and I even get my statements sent to my e-mail address.

"What's great about banking online is that I have constant access to my accounts – I can log on as many times as I want to check my balance, so it's easier to keep an eye on how much money I don't have. I rarely go over my overdraft limit any more, so it's also meant less bank charges.

"I've recently decided to be more financially responsible, so I have been logging on to some financial websites to find out what I should be doing to improve my money situation. **www.fool.co.uk** is a great site, with straightforward and funny advice. The fool site thinks I should be freezing my credit cards into a block of ice to stop me using them!

"I tend to move my credit card debt onto different cards every few months to make the most of the cheapest interest rates. **www.moneysupermarket.com** is great for comparison shopping for cards, because it compares insurance rates but also spells out the small print for each card.

"Once I get my financial act together, I'll also be getting a savings account online, and maybe in the distant future I'll get a cyber-mortgage or even buy shares!"

Virtual banks

You'll get the best rates of all at the new internet banks. Exclusively online, with no high street branches, these new banks don't have to pay for a high street presence and, as a result, can offer you some excellent deals. They also can offer extra benefits, such as e-mail addresses and shopping sites. Check out **www.cahoot.com**, **www.if.com**, **www.first-e.com**, and **www.smile.com** to experience the benefits of virtual banking.

It may be worth looking into moving your accounts to these banks simply to take advantage of these better rates. By taking a completely fresh approach to the whole banking system, they also offer innovative new financial products such as single accounts to hold all your savings and loan accounts together. They don't have branches, but they do have staff available, on the phone and on e-mail, 24 hours a day. Don't be put off by the quirky names and don't worry that your savings are at risk. The virtual banks have been set up by established financial institutions. **www.egg.com**, for example, is owned by The Prudential.

It's not just banks going online, all kinds of financial providers now work through the internet. From arranging insurance, loans and mortgages to managing your savings accounts and credit cards, you'll be amazed how quick and easy it can be. Your bank may also offer you extra incentives, like free internet access, to encourage you to use their online service. For credit cards, try **www.egg.com**, **www.marbles.com**, and **www.capitalone.co.uk**.

Security

Although it may feel less safe than real-world banking, the banks are extremely security-conscious. They have virtually uncrackable encryption systems to protect their data (such as your bank balances and transactions). There have been stories of hackers getting into banks and finding out customers' details, but it is also true that a real-world bank account is equally vulnerable to such hacking.

However, it may be possible to compromise your own security by being careless with your passwords, so treat them as you would your cashpoint PIN. You will be given a security code and a PIN number or a password. You may also be asked additional questions, such as your mother's maiden name or your birthday, making it doubly difficult for anyone else to get it.

Financial advice

Another way you can improve your financial affairs is to log on to one of the many advice sites and take advantage of their wealth of useful information on everything from investment tips and writing a will to getting the latest bank account interest rates. You'll find interesting articles, news and discussion groups to join, comparative tables for an at-a-glance guide to the best credit card offers and more. If you use an internet portal as your gateway to the net, it may have a money section, making it one of the best places to start your search for the information you need. Log on to **www.fool.co.uk**, **www.ftyourmoney.com**, or **www.handbag.com/finance**.

Mortgage savings

Use the internet to help you find the best mortgage deal around and you could save thousands. Many people only change mortgage when they move house, even though the figures show that it pays to switch mortgage every few years. Even if you have to pay a redemption penalty, it's possible to make big monthly savings. **www.charcolonline.co.uk**, **www.hotmortgage.co.uk** and **www.moneygator.com** offer advice on the best deals around.

"I'm about to get married, and at the same time change jobs, and move from London back up north to Leeds, so I'm rushed off my feet! My future husband and I are having to sell our flat and buy a house too. It's a nightmare – everyone has an opinion when you're buying a home. Whether it's the place, the type of place, how much to pay, even how to pay. It makes truly helpful, independent advice all the more valuable, wherever you find it. Especially since I've got no spare time at the moment.

"Luckily, the internet has been a tremendous help, particularly on the money side of things – there's so much to help with every step of buying a home, and it's so easy to find. Shopping around for the best rates is so much faster now. From mortgage calculators to lender comparisons, everything is at your fingertips. Using sites like **www.moneygator.com** and **www.fool.co.uk** we avoided the countless sessions with over-eager advisers telling us their discounted variables were far better value than a capped rate repayment. Simple, straightforward and easy to play with, the calculators and comparison tables showed us what we could – and couldn't – afford. It's just a shame the net can't help with all the packing!"

Online share trading

Once, you needed a living, breathing stockbroker to buy and sell your shares. But, with the advent of the internet, you can connect directly to the markets yourself, research investment opportunities or take advantage of one of the many affordable, convenient online share services. Over 25% of all sharetrading now takes place through the net. Take a look at some of the online trading sites like **www.etrade.co.uk** and **www.selftrade.co.uk**.

Thanks to the internet, there's now a whole new world of information, inspiration, advice and services available at the click of a mouse. It's waiting there for you – so get out there and use it! But remember, it's important to keep up to date with the latest developments on the net. That way, you'll be ready to take advantage of the wonderful time and money-saving initiatives as they arrive. If you're looking forward to paying your bills from your mobile phone, watch this space!

You know it's time to log on when:

- You've spent your lunch hour standing in line at the bank
- Your money is not making you any money
- Your taxes are in a muddle – check out **www.inlandrevenue.gov.uk**

Money sites

General financial sites

www.iii.com, Interactive Investor International, is one of the most popular UK financial websites.

www.find.co.uk is a good starting-point, an internet directory for everything finance-related, with links to all financial sectors.

www.fsa.gov.uk is the place to go if you need help with your financial rights, it's the home page of the Financial Services Authority.

www.ft.com and **www.ftyourmoney.com** are both from the Financial Times, with all the latest news and information, and a customisable 'mymoney' section.

www.thisismoney.com is a comprehensive site from the Daily Mail, with easy to use advice and information on your personal finances.

www.fool.co.uk is a fun site covering all aspects of managing your money, including bulletin boards so you can find out what people really think of the service they get!

www.mrscohen.com provides advice from the inimitable Mrs. Cohen, with a straightforward, easy-to-use approach to financial advice.

High street and virtual banks and building societies

www.abbeynational.co.uk
www.alliance-leicester.co.uk
www.barclays.co.uk
www.bradford-bingley.co.uk
www.cahoot.com
www.citibank.co.uk
www.co-operativebank.co.uk
www.egg.co.uk

www.firstdirect.co.uk
www.first-e.com
www.halifax.co.uk
www.hsbc.com
www.imbd.com – the internet savings bank.
www.lloydstsb.co.uk
www.nationwide.co.uk
www.natwest.co.uk
www.pru.co.uk – The Prudential.
www.rbs.co.uk – the Royal Bank of Scotland.
www.smile.co.uk – Smile internet bank.
www.virgin-direct.co.uk
www.woolwich.co.uk
www.if.co.uk is the 'Intelligent Finance' internet bank.

Mortgages and insurance

www.charcolonline.co.uk offers independent lending advice, on
mortgages, pensions, investments and insurance.
www.homequote.co.uk will give you free insurance quotes for your
home and contents insurance.
www.screentrade.co.uk will search out the cheapest quote across
all categories of insurance, and you can buy your policy online as well.
www.moneysupermarket.com lets you shop around a virtual
supermarket of financial products.

Credit cards

www.americanexpress.co.uk
www.barclaycard.co.uk
www.capitalone.co.uk
www.dinersclub.com
www.egg.com
www.goldfish.com

www.marbles.com
www.cahoot.com
www.mbna.co.uk

Investing

www.etrade.co.uk
www.barclays-stockbrokers.co.uk – the stockbroking arm of
Barclays Bank.
www.sharepeople.com
www.xest.com – execution-only online share trading.
www.comdirect.co.uk
www.schwab-worldwide.com/europe – the European arm of the
world's biggest online stockbroker.
www.selftrade.co.uk
www.sharexpress.co.uk
www.nasdaq.com – monitor the world's technology stock market
from your desktop.
www.londonstockexchange.com has the latest share prices and
details of all stockbrokers on the exchange.

Tax

www.inlandrevenue.gov.uk is the homepage of tax, for you to get
help with all your tax issues, with links to other Government tax sites.
www.tax.org.uk is the homepage of the Chartered Institute of
Taxation, with a list of all UK tax advisers.
http://listen.to/taxman has a very handy PAYE calculator, to show
you exactly how much you should be taking home.

Chapter 16

Good Parenting

Parenting is a thrilling (and challenging) adventure, filled with lots of changes and expectations. In the past, new parents relied on their doctor, family and friends, or books from the library for advice. New mothers were often prisoners in their own home. Stressed-out parents had nowhere to turn when things hit crisis point. Shopping with a pram, or worse, a runaway child, could be a nightmare, going into labour a terrifying journey into the unknown, and finding the right school a matter of luck, rather than judgement.

But today, whether you're planning a baby, coping with a newborn or have a house full of mini commandos (aka toddlers), the internet can give you an astonishing amount of information, support, useful contacts and just plain fun. There are thousands of sites, offering practical help and advice, great shopping deals, vital support networks and shared experiences from parents all over the world. From the moment you decide that parenthood is for you, to the day you wave your darlings goodbye, put the resources of the internet to good use and you'll never look back. To start your internet parenting journey, try **www.mumsnet.com**.

Web Life – Parenting online

- Trying times. It often takes time to conceive, so help ease the strain by getting some expert advice or signing up for the new e-conception services on **www.motherandbaby.co.uk**

- Parenting advice. Even before you start a family the internet is full of practical advice and statistics on the responsibility of being a parent and how to give your baby the start ever. Try **www.ukparents.co.uk**

- Expert advice. With advisory panels and online experts you can get advice and help to support you throughout your pregnancy and raising the baby at **www.babyworld.co.uk**

- Feeding time. From breastfeeding to weaning, find the answers online at **www.breastfeeding.co.uk**

- Nameless. Choosing the name for your baby can be a difficult task, so why not get a little help online with the biggest directory of names from around the world on **www.babycentre.co.uk**

- Best buys. With interactive guides on all the best tried and tested babyseats, pushchairs, carseats to nappies, you can buy everything you need online from favourites like **www.mothercare.com**

E-conception

The internet can do many wonderful things, but did you know it can help you conceive? Forget expensive ovulation testing kits, the messaging service on your mobile phone can alert you when you're about to enter your most fertile few days. As Sarah Stone, the website editor of **www.motherandbaby.co.uk** explains, their e-conception service lets you know by e-mail or text message when that special time has come. Just visit the site and enter in the first day of your last period and the length of your menstrual cycle. It's got to be worth a try, just for the fun of it if nothing else.

Case Study
Rachel Sharman

"I gave birth to my first baby, Kitty, about eight months ago. Because I was pregnant for the first time I didn't know what to expect, and if the feelings I was having were normal. The net was a great help, because I could look anything up to reassure myself, without having to ask my doctor or my friends.

"I also got help with naming Kitty, and got a laugh out of all the bizarre names I could have called her. I'm looking up baby-weaning recipes now that she's older. I also use the net for shopping, since it's so much easier to get online than to drive to the shops, find mother and baby parking, and struggle with collapsing the pram to get it in and out of the car.

"The net's helped me keep in touch with the world, so that I haven't completely disappeared into a cloud of baby-powder! I've recently started working again, from home with e-mail. It's nice to be able to communicate normally, rather than in the sing-song voice you forget you're doing! Our postnatal group keeps in contact via e-mail, arranging coffee mornings and organising baby massage and baby swimming lessons."

Boy or girl?

Did you know that the shape of your bump can tell you if you're having a boy or a girl? Have you heard that the 'position' in which you conceive can make a difference? There are some often-hilarious myths that determine the sex of your baby. Just for fun, take a look at **www.chinagold.com** and see what the ancient Chinese have to say about it.

A fun way to find out about your baby before he or she is born is to work out their horoscope. Try **www.horoscopes.com** so that you're prepared!

If you're stuck for names, get some ideas on the net. There are lots of babynaming sites, but the best place to start is probably Yahoo's own site, at **http://babynames.pregnancy.yahoo.com** which has over 10,000 names, grouped into categories. Or try **www.babynamer.com**, for a more American perspective.

Nine months of fun

With the internet you have your own team of pregnancy and birth experts, from midwifes and obstetricians to other labouring mothers, on call 24 hours a day. Put the power of the net behind you through all the different stages of pregnancy, from the morning sickness of the first trimester to the birth itself. **www.pregnancycalendar.com** will walk you through those amazing nine months, showing you how your baby grows and how your body changes. You can share in the unique and personal experiences of others through online diaries at **www.emmasdiary.co.uk**, which gives you a week-by-week guide to pregnancy, birth and labour in a diary format.

At **www.babyworld.co.uk** you have instant access to doctors, midwives and fertility experts, as well as a vast archive of frequently asked questions and answers. Giving you practical advice on diet, rest and useful product reviews, **www.iparenting.com** has a daily pregnancy calendar with your own 'countdown' to the Big Day. The man in your life also has his own section in this site with lots of light-hearted advice and encouragement to stop him feeling left out.

Labour Day

You can prepare for the birth well in advance, with a visit to **www.childbirth.org** which has real life birth experiences as well as an overview of all the birth options available (focusing on the natural rather than the medical). The women's portals as well as the major baby sites all contain lively, friendly advice that can make the whole experience less frightening and much more rewarding.

You're not alone

One of the best opportunities the internet offers you is the chance to chat to other couples about parenting issues, sharing your experiences, getting answers to your questions, and finding support from people in the same position as you. Log on to **www.ukparents.co.uk** and put your mind at rest!

Giving your baby the right start in life and enjoying that special time is so important for all the family. We all need a little advice on how to tell whether a baby is off colour or needs urgent attention. By logging on you can get advice on weaning, **www.breastfeeding.co.uk** provides some great hints and tips all backed by experts.

"There is an expanse of information and facilities for mothers on the net, which means that a woman's life at home can be more interesting. Ordering things from the net can free up more time to do the fun things in life, like coffee mornings with other mothers and sprogs! The internet also helps with just keeping a hand in the office environment, working from home.

"When I became pregnant and got to the stage where I needed to buy things for the baby, I was sure that I did not want the run of the mill, high street shop things. I am the type of person who does not like walking down the road and seeing people either wearing or having the same stuff as myself. Buying baby things from the internet has meant I can get individual clothes from anywhere in the world, and it's still less stressful than going down the high street when you're eight months pregnant!

"A friend of mine recommended a website called Alice Hart, **www.alicehart.co.uk**, and I took a look at the site, and ordered a Moses basket. From here the scope grew – a buggy ordered from Holland, clothes from IKKS from France, at **www.ikks.com**, even down to a pair of sheepskin booties from the Alps! For the more practical and essential disposable stuff I ordered from Mothercare, and was amazed that the following day things were on my doorstep – it was so easy!"

Later on

Did you know it costs more than £70 per week to maintain a four-year-old outside of London? Look at **www.ukparents.co.uk** to find out more facts on the reality behind childcare. **www.childcarelink.org.uk** has details of all your childcare options, and links to local, Government-approved carers.

It's important to do your research when checking and applying for local schools – the net makes this research so much easier. **www.upmystreet.co.uk** will have details of all the schools in your area. **www.goodschoolsguide.com** will help you find out more about them.

The internet also has a wealth of education resources which are perfect for kids, no matter what their age. See the Education online chapter for more details.

A little humour and advice is always at hand on the net, helping to guide you through the constantly changing role of being a good parent.

You know it's time to log on when:

- You're worrying day and night about doing the right things during pregnancy
- The only names you can think of read like the cast of Eastenders
- You're being sick every morning and want to know when it will end
- You need some independent advice on the benefits of breast and bottle-feeding

Sites for parents

General parenting sites

www.mumsnet.com – an online community for shared parenting advice. Share your own tips, or read what works for other parents.
www.parents.org.uk – for parents with primary school-aged kids, with debates on topical issues, reviews and links.
www.practicalparent.org.uk is a one-stop resource for parents, focusing on child behaviour and development.
www.allaboutparents.com
www.ukmums.co.uk has chatrooms and forums for all UK parents.
www.e-mum.com, the UK site for busy mums and dads, including a regular newsletter.
www.parents-news.co.uk is an information site for families.
www.motherandbaby.co.uk is the website of Mother and Baby magazine.
www.childcare-info.co.uk has reliable information on childcare-related topics, including useful addresses and tips on choosing the right childcare.
www.nurserydirect.co.uk has nursery products at discounted prices.

Pregnancy sites

www.babycentre.co.uk Can't think of a name for your baby? Try this site for options in 43 languages, including the meanings behind the names.
www.chinagold.com Try this ancient Chinese method to determine the sex of your baby.
www.babyworld.co.uk. This information-packed site has plenty of material for dads-to-be and the diary of a woman undergoing fertility treatment.

www.motherandbaby.co.uk is a personalised e-conception and pregnancy planner as well as a week-by-week health check.

www.fitpregnancy.com. This e-mail service gives you the answers to your questions and the chance to chat to other mums-to-be.

www.homebirth.org.uk and **www.homebirth.net** are good sites if you're looking into having a homebirth.

www.activebirthcentre.com plan an 'active birth', with a list of birth teachers and details of birthing pool hire.

www.emmasdiary.co.uk is a personal insight into the pregnancy of Emma and her friends, filled with advice and shared experiences. Backed by the Royal College of General Practitioners.

www.thebabyregistry.co.uk has free e-mail, pregnancy help and advice for new mothers.

Education sites

www.kidsmatter.co.uk focuses on expert educational advice for parents of kids aged 0-11.

www.schoolsnet.com is the UK's number one education portal, with a comprehensive school directory and educational resources for kids, parents and teachers.

www.schoolbusuk.com will let you find out about any school in the UK, with full National League tables.

Maternity wear on the net

www.bumpmaternity.com is a great site selling fun maternity and baby clothes.

www.mothercare.com sells maternity wear and baby products

www.bloomingmarvellous.co.uk sells fashionable clothes for expectant mothers.

www.jojomamanbebe.com offers beautifully-made French clothes.

Chapter 17

Kids Online

The geeky image of young 'net heads' has long gone. As the NOP family research shows, today's kids consider themselves clever and lucky to use the internet. From a very early age, technology is playing a part in their everyday lives. In fact, the children of the information age grow up knowing more about technology than their parents did and often teach other members of the family about the internet.

Kids have increasing access to technology too, with over 40% enjoying internet access from home. Bedrooms are becoming high tech dens, with TVs, videos, mobile phones, and even personal computers! If you do have home internet access, make sure that older family members do not monopolise it. It's also important to show kids how to search and surf, so they can find information quickly and easily.

But while kids use 'homework' as the number one reason to persuade parents to get a computer with internet access, they use the net for much more besides. When kids log on they find a whole host of reasons to like the internet. It is informative and fun, the most popular activities being education, information, communication and games. Access is still more likely at home than at school and still takes up a small proportion of time (1.7 hours per week) compared to TV (21.3 hours per week).

Case Study
Lucy Whitaker, aged 7

"I use the internet at school and at home, for about 3 hours a week. I don't like it when it is slow, and when I can't find what I want to look at. But I really like it when I get sent e-mails. My uncle always sends me e-cards on my birthday! I also use the internet to e-mail to my friends and family. I send e-mails to a friend that I met on holiday in France, and I e-mail to my friend in Spain.

"At school I look at sites which help me in the subjects we are doing, like Living Library at **www.livlib.eduweb.co.uk**. The one I am doing now is **www.clarkehall.com** because we are going on a school visit to see what it was like to live in Tudor times. At home my favourite site is **www.yahooligans.com**. I look for topics that I am learning about at school, and there are some good games to play on the site as well. On the **www.bbc.co.uk** site I look for programmes I like to watch on TV, and I also find Tweenies and Bob the Builder and download the music for my little sister Rebecca."

Web Life – Kids' interests online

- Loads of information – as the biggest library in the world the internet's a wealth of fascinating facts and figures, graphics, photographs, video and documents. Being able to find information is the top scoring reason for kids going online. Look up the online encyclopaedias **www.encarta.msn.com** and **www.britannica.co.uk**

- Educational benefits – when it comes to homework or revision, you can get your questions answered, search on any subject you need and find really useful resources for exams, further education and careers. Try **www.homeworkhigh.com**, for homework help for all ages

- Hot search – Search engines are fast, easy to use and show you the best sites, such as **www.ajkids.com**, **www.yahooligans.com**, and **www.altavista.com**

- Active interactive – with live interviews and chatrooms, plus a constant supply of new information, the net comes to life. **www.planit4kids.com** and **www.eplay.com**

- Playtime – giving access to the latest games, the net's got the edge over consoles. Plus, with music, film and celebrity news and gossip, kids can turn their desks into complete entertainment centres. **www.bonus.com** and **www.galaxykids.com**

- E-mail appeal – e-mailing friends and family is a popular activity with over half of all kids online

- Buying online – 36% of internet kids have looked for something to buy and 16% have actually bought something, with 78% using their parents credit card. Interestingly, most do contribute or pay back the cost. Source: Wave 4 NOP family survey

Top marks

Getting good marks in coursework and exams used to be a teenage worry. Today those exam nerves hit early. In the UK, kids are sitting their first SAT exams at seven with the next set at eleven. With all this pressure to do well, the internet offers a real advantage.

The internet changes the lives of kids with limited access to books and libraries. It opens up a whole new world of learning. Even before school, kids can play and try new activities on interactive fun sites, like **www.bbc.co.uk/littlekids**. The internet makes learning fun, interesting and most important, interactive. Kids can find out facts from around the world and e-mail them to friends.

Once at school there are some excellent child-friendly search engines and sites that can help with schoolwork. **www.topmarks.co.uk** is a site that helps kids search for information from the educational websites. From help with maths to specific information on volcanoes, this site will help. Channel 4 has a useful homework helper, at **www.homeworkhigh.co.uk**, with answers to over 15,000 questions, covering all subjects and lets you post a question if you can't find the answer. Or try the BBC's homework help site at **www.bbc.co.uk/education/schools**.

A great way to encourage kids to start using the net (not that they need much encouragement!) is to find sites on subjects they love. For example, Harry Potter has lots of different websites. Try starting at **www.bloomsbury.com/harrypotter**, or just do a web search and see what you can turn up. Other children's authors with web pages are Anne Fine www.annefine.co.uk, Dr. Seuss, **www.seussville.com**, and Roald Dahl, **www.roalddahl.org**.

Tweenies

The tweenies, as researchers have called them, are between 8 and 13, in that transition phase from childhood to adolescence. They're computer literate, fashionable and have spending power, which they exercise in their choice of CDs and clothes. They also have a sense of responsibility and independence, realising early that it is important to do well at school.

Tweenies are well aware of the benefits of the internet. They use it to help them do homework and, in the case of girls, gossip and chat online. Sites aimed specifically at them, like **www.cosmogirl.com** and **www.agirlsworld.com** have the latest glittery bits, while sites of TV shows such as Buffy the Vampire Slayer, **www.buffy.com**, and Hollyoaks, **www.hollyoaks.com**, enjoy a cult tweenie following.

Hot Tips – Kids' safety on the net

* Filtering software – this can ensure that access is limited to safe sites. Your ISP may provide this service or you could try software such as Net Nanny. But determined kids will always find a way, so either make sure they are supervised or be prepared! Try **www.cyberangels.com** and **www.netnanny.com** for the latest updates and to buy filtering software

* Personal information – kids can be trusting and need to be told not to give out personal information, such as addresses and telephone numbers online

* Online privacy protection – new legislation requires commercial websites to get parental permission before collecting and using information from children

* Credit cards – if you let your kids use your cards, lay down the rules and enforce them!

See the *Surfing Safely* chapter for more information

Case Study
Sarah Brown, aged 12

"Using the internet scores highly on my list of interests. The wide range of subjects available helps me with my homework. I surf the net about three to four times a week for about an hour, more if I am lucky and have research homework. The main sites I use are **www.bbc.co.uk**, **www.ask-jeeves.co.uk** and **www.yahoo.co.uk** I have found loads of information for History, Geography and Art. It's earned me lots of house points, so I must have done something right! Although we have a library of books at home the net puts far more information at my fingertips.

"It's easy to find the latest news about my favourite bands. When I can twist Mum or Dad's arm we can buy a CD, and it saves them money too! Mostly we have bought from **www.audiostreet.co.uk**.

"I discovered **www.anythingleft-handed.co.uk** – being left-handed, some of their products have really helped me, especially the ruler, people just don't realise how awkward a normal ruler is!

"Last summer I went to an international jamboree. The website was available before the event so you could see what was planned and make contact with others. I e mailed girls from Sweden and The Isle of Man. While I was there people could look to see what was going on while at home. Mum and Dad could see a web-cam of parts of the site.

"E-mailing is brilliant as you can keep in touch with friends and family over the world in a matter of minutes – far better than snail mail! E-cards are designed for different occasions and many styles too. **www.hotmail.com** is a fabulous free e-mailing system, I recommend it. The one thing I don't really use is chatlines as I'm only 12 and have heard of many incidents when people are on there to annoy others."

Safety online

With the internet, kids can prepare for adolescence and adult life. They can get a broader view of the world, build up their confidence, take responsibility for their studies and experiment with their identity. It may be worrying to think of them seeing the darker side of life though the internet, but then again, we have to set them free.

That doesn't mean parents can't put safety nets in place. It is worth taking a little time to set some house rules and show your kids how to surf safely. The NOP family study revealed that one in three children are happy to give out their address and personal details online, especially in return for free samples, gifts and information. So while children might be internet savvy, they need some lessons in safety.

Bullying help from the net

Unfortunately bullying is a common problem for many kids, leading to feelings of isolation and despair at any age. The internet provides an ideal way for kids to get help, and also for concerned parents to research a solution. A good UK bullying site is **www.bullying.co.uk**. It has help for parents and kids, including legal advice. Kids can e-mail their problems or read the problem page. It also has links to other useful anti-bullying resources, sites like **www.childline.org.uk**, and **www.nspcc.org.uk**. **www.educationunlimited.co.uk** is The Guardian's education portal with good articles to help with bullying problems; **www.parents.dfee.gov.uk** is the Government's own site dealing with bullying and similar educational issues.

Kids' web skills

The internet has so much to offer to
kids, from help with homework to advice on growing up, it
is essential that we help all kids discover its benefits sooner
rather than later. Every child should experience the learning
powers of the internet, otherwise we create a digital divide between
those who log on and those who do not.

The young who do not have access to the internet will lack the skills
and tools they need to take part in this new Information Economy.
The digital have-nots will be excluded from many of the skilled jobs.
While girls enjoy logging on, they have little interest in the technicalities
of how the net works, compared with boys. This may influence their
career choices, we need to build more confidence and interest in the
internet at an earlier age. The Government and industry are attempting
to do this and there is plenty you can do to help.

With the increasing availability of access in libraries,
internet cafes and schools there are lots of other ways
to link up, as the directory at the end of this book
shows. It is not essential to have internet access at
home, although this is the most popular place to surf,
and possibly the easiest way to monitor your kids.

The truth is that if you have kids you cannot let them miss
out on this fantastic resource. The internet really does
make learning fun and it is flexible enough to offer
information on anything, from religious education to rabbits.
Your kids have the opportunity to be in control of their
entertainment, learning, friendships and the tricky process of
growing up in a wired world.

You know it's time to log on when:

- You have read the latest Harry Potter ten times
- You can recite every word to the Simpsons
- You need to brush up on your french or physics
- You realise you could be missing out on something interesting
- You're worried your kid's getting bullied, and don't know what to do about it

Websites for kids

Kids' starting points on the net

www.yahooligans.com is Yahoo's kids portal, which is carefully filtered to make sure its content is suitable.
www.surfnetkids.com
www.bbc.co.uk/webguide has a weekly selection of the three best kids' websites. There's something new every week.
www.girltech.com is a US site for girls to encourage them to be more confident on the internet, with a girl-powered search engine, chat rooms, games and links to other sites.

Kids' search sites

It's important that everyone is able to search the net quickly. Kids' search sites are the ideal way for children to develop searching skills early. These sites also return exclusively child-suitable material, so they're perfect if you can't always supervise your kids' online time.
www.ajkids.com is the Ask Jeeves net directory, geared and filtered for kids.

www.yahooligans.com is a keyword search engine (among other things) just for kids, including links to useful websites.
www.about.com/kids is the child-friendly section of the **www.about.com** search directory.
Search engines like **www.google.com** and **www.altavista.com** also have filters you can set to screen out inappropriate content.

Kids' TV sites

www.nick.com is an excellent kids website from Nickelodeon.
www.foxkids.co.uk is the Fox Kids network online.
www.cartoonnetwork.com.
www.citv.co.uk is the homepage of Children's ITV.
www.bbc.co.uk/cbbc is the site for Children's BBC.
www.warnerbros.com.

Education sites

www.wsu.edu/druniverse will answer all the tough kids' questions for you. Kids can ask Dr Universe himself or look through the archived questions.
www.beakman.com
www.discovery.com, from the American Discovery channel, has a great kids' section on all things scientific.
www.nationalgeographic.com/kids is a mine of useful geographical information.
www.funbrain.com is a fun learning site for the under-sixes, with word and number games and a search facility.
www.topmarks.co.uk is a search engine for finding educational websites, helping kids find information on all their subjects.
www.eduweb.co.uk is an education website for teachers and pupils with a carefully-filtered directory of educational webpages and internet resources.
www.atschool.co.uk is a learning portal for primary school-aged kids, with good resources for parents too.

www.virtualschool.co.uk sends courses by e-mail in all the main subjects, plus interactive help with expert input.

www.edview.com is a great educational directory with kids links, grouped into subject areas.

www.funschool.com is a US site with free online educational games for kids of all ages.

www.schoolzone.co.uk has 30,000 free resources for kids, compiled by UK teachers.

www.learningstore.co.uk is a comprehensive e-commerce site selling all kinds of educational and reference software, for kids and adult learning.

www.wordcentral.com is a vocabulary building site.

Activities and things to do

www.beano.co.uk for games, chat and all your favourite characters from the Beano.

www.kidsevents.co.uk has loads of suggestions on how to keep the kids happy, like days out and events.

www.yucky.com and **www.grossology.org** have the disgusting stuff that kids love: two revolting sites with all things slimy!

www.winniethepooh.co.uk is great for younger kids.

www.mamamedia.com is a bright, creative site where kids can make their own animations, cards and drawings.

www.moma.org/artsafari is a site to help kids explore the Museum of Modern Art in New York.

www.nhm.ac.uk is the Natural History Museum online.

www.sciencemuseum.org.uk has information on science that's perfect for kids.

www.planit4kids.com has plenty of ideas for a day out.

Chapter 18

Teen Power

Over a million UK teenage girls are online, they are one of the biggest growing groups of internet users. These girls are the empowered net generation; teens everywhere are making the most of being online. As girls start to become more interested in IT, the digital gender gap will hopefully soon become a thing of the past. The net fits increasingly comfortably into girls' lives, enabling them to feel connected. Going online to chat, to e-mail, to be in touch – communicating online is a real part of their lives.

Online magazines, e-zines, shopping and music draw a big youth audience; with teenage girls such avid surfers, there are lots of sites catering to their needs. E-mail and Instant Messaging are among the most popular uses of the net for teenage girls – chatting with friends and boyfriends makes the most of the need to communicate.

The magic of the internet goes beyond this as it plays right into the heart of teenage life. Being a teenager is not easy. Just as the hormones are raging, the pressure of relationships, homework, betrayed friendships and finding out who you are all becomes too much. It's amazing how logging on can also help in those delicate phases of growing up. At the click of a mouse you can find someone that really understands you, to share experiences, get advice and have a laugh. Chatrooms and problem pages can truly help make you find the answers and help with growing up, and you can be as anonymous as you want.

Web Life – Teen life online

* Send an e-mail – the essential way to keep in touch, make new friends and communicate. **www.hotmail.com** is one of the easiest ways to get e-mail

* Get chatty – head for a chatroom and try out a new identity, meet new friends and have fun at **www.thej.net**

* Do your homework – the best way to do research and get hold of any piece of information you need. Try **www.gcse.com**, or **www.a-levels.co.uk**

* Get your problems sorted – no need to be scared of talking about your most embarrassing problems online now at **www.youth2youth.co.uk**

* Listen to the latest music – catch up with the gossip on your favourite stars, download free MP3s. Try **www.napster.com** and **www.nme.com**

* Read an e-zine – the essential way to log into the most up-to-date gossip, trends and fashions. Log on to **www.chickclick.com**

* Be a fashion victim – do some online purchasing and get hold of the best bargains and the coolest brands. TopShop's website is at **www.tops.co.uk**

Case Study
Rachel Dugdale, 17

Rachel Dugdale has an experience of the internet typical for many young women. "A few years ago I started using it to look for information on physics for school. Then when my friends got e-mail we started to use that a lot. I access the internet almost daily, either from my school network or from home in the evenings. The internet makes getting in contact with people so much easier: I subscribe to a number of e-groups which helps me keep in touch with larger groups of people all over the world. I also keep in touch with my boyfriend via a daily e-mail. He lives in Oxford, while I'm in Preston, so it would be a pretty inconvenient, long-distance relationship without the internet."

Rachel also has a good idea of what the internet means for her future. "Hopefully it will mean I can work from home a lot of the time, and perhaps my partner will be able to do that also. This means I could think of having kids without having to entirely give up work. Before this occurred to me, I would never have considered having kids. The ability to work from home and the possibility of communicating via the internet means it's possible to do things which otherwise wouldn't have been thought of.

"The internet has made the world a smaller place, with more individuals having close connections to other countries and nationalities. The fear of the unknown is gradually going away, and will be replaced by a greater commitment to international peace."

Information hungry

Finding information and getting help with homework are positive reasons teenage girls get online. The net is useful and convenient, easier and more fun to use than the library. There are even specialist homework websites, which enable you to get interactive help if you're struggling with your schoolwork.

Case Study
Nicola Mason, 17

Nicola Mason, 17, uses the internet every day for e-mail and research, getting online at school and at home. "It has helped me a lot to gain knowledge for current homework. If I didn't have the internet, I would find it really difficult to do my assignments! I think the internet has made a lot of good changes to everyday life... it is a constant time-saver for anyone looking for any kind of information."

Integrating the internet into your working schedule will make learning a lot more enjoyable. You can also use it to research your future possibilities – try **www.ucas.co.uk** to check out what's available at university, or **www.push.co.uk** for the inside scoop on what student life is really like. If you're going to have a gap year, research the many possibilities for travelling, or working, on the internet, at **www.gapyear.com**.

Pick a fun e-mail address from the huge choice at www.another.com, so you can let people know who you really are! It's free, and you can pick more than one address to e-mail your friends with.

Shopping sprees

Stories of teenagers spending
thousands shopping on the internet
may be more hype than reality. Even
so, the reality is that teens have significant
disposable income from their parents and jobs. With the average
annual income for 14-16 year olds being £600 a year, teens have
significant online purchasing power. Even in their early teens, girls are
active consumers and like to take responsibility for their own purchases.
Although it may only start with sweets and chocolates, when girls hit late
teens over 60% buy their own clothes. The internet gives greater access
to shops, and with no travel limitations teens can buy the latest fashions,
music, software, and games. Getting a good deal online is also attractive:
a KPMG study found that price was the most important reason for
shopping online for half the teens surveyed. Although e-commerce is
attracting the attention and the hard earned cash there is still one major
barrier: how to make the payment.

The good news is that online purchasing no longer depends on borrowing
your parents' credit cards. So worries about wild teenage online shopping
sprees may soon be a thing of the past, with the launch of a number of
schemes aimed at attracting teen cash. One of the digital cash schemes
for under-18 shoppers is Smartcreds. This is a pay-as-you-go net
shopping card, which you can then use in a range of approved online
shops. The Smartcreds card works in the same way as a pay-as-you-go
phone card: money is deposited and then the card holder can use
the credits. Log onto **www.uksmart.co.uk** and **www.rools.co.uk** or one
of the similar payment sites listed at the end of this chapter to check out
progress, and open an account.

Web Facts – UK girls are net aware

- Teenagers are the world's fastest growing internet population. According to Computer Economics, 77 million teenagers will be online by 2005

- The number of girls 12-17 using the internet worldwide increased by 125% from 1999 to 2000, and this growth is set to accelerate!

- UK teens have grown up with technology and so have high internet awareness and usage. The NOP family 'kids.net' research shows that 1.06 million 6-16-year-olds use the net in the UK

- The average computer usage by UK girls in 1999 was 1.7 hours a week from home and 0.6 hours from school

- Teens' most popular use of the internet activities are e-mail, chatting, games, music and research

la pomme

Music online

Teen culture for decades has been based around music, a way of defining your identity, friendships and filling nights. Pop, house, garage, techno, hardcore – teenagers in bedrooms everywhere are chilling out with the newest sounds. The biggest growth area of the internet is the trade in MP3 music files, which enable you to download CD-quality music tracks for free, and play them from your computer or an MP3 player. Go to **www.lycos.com** for the best MP3 directory. **www.napster.com**, the biggest file-sharing agent on the net also lets you access other people's MP3 files. However, make sure you are aware of copyright issues before you do this, as you might be breaking the law. **www.bpi.co.uk** has all the latest updates on music copyright law and the internet.

For poptastic gossip and the latest chart news, check out **www.worldpop.com** and find out the latest on your favourite bands. Other good music sites include **www.nme.com**, **www.music.com**, and **www.ejay.co.uk**.

Then there are the virtual pop stars, manufactured bands that only exist as cartoons on the internet. The latest virtual band is Gorillaz, hoping to be noticed for their music not their appearance. Damon Albarn from Blur is involved, so they can expect some success. Decide for yourself at **www.gorillaz.com**.

Techno savvy

Today's teens are technologically and brand savvy. They know what is cool and will find it for themselves online. Sites have to have street cred, be humourous, open and diverse. Animation and design that capture emotions are appealing, but they have to be fast to download. The mainstream media is too conservative, the net is fun, a bit wild and wacky and great for communicating. With the new generation devices to access to the internet being more accessible, cheaper and cool – they have big teen appeal. Mobile internet, interactive TV, personal digital assistants are predicted to attract even more teens online. Although many girls do see a downside to the net with the threat of online exploitation by adults, they are also mature enough to deal with unsafe situations.

The time when all UK teens are online may not be far away. Being connected is becoming a way of life for the net generation of females, especially with the rise in text messaging, exchanging e-mails, and with more girls using the internet as an invaluable educational resource. Girls already spend more time online than boys do. With more girls logging on, the next stage is to use this to knock down the barriers to girls going into high tech jobs. It is not enough to just log on, we have to encourage more girls to relate the benefits of the internet to their future careers.

> **You know it's time to log on when:**
>
> - You've got an embarrassing problem you need to share
> - You want to cram in as much revision as possible
> - You want to keep in touch with your boyfriend without a massive phone bill

Top sites for teens

Teen portals and chat sites

www.girlynation.com is a US site with beauty articles and tips. You can even chat live to beauty experts!

www.razzberry.com is a US community site for girls, with links and great articles on everything you could think of.

www.bolt.com an online 'hangout', this huge US site is the ultimate online club for teenagers.

www.trouble.co.uk, from Trouble TV, is a fun site with links to TV and entertainment-related subjects.

www.brit-teen.com, a UK portal specialising in entertainment, with articles, links and interactive features.

www.mykindaplace.com is a popular UK magazine-style portal for girls, with problem pages, reviews and chat.

www.teentalk.org.uk has chatrooms and problem pages answered by Dr Teen.

www.teenfront.com, run exclusively by teenagers, this is teens' first stop on the net.

www.ukteen.com has message boards and live chatrooms for younger teenagers.

www.thej.net is one of the biggest European teen sites, focusing on chat.

www.bbc.co.uk/so is the teen portal from the BBC, with links to all your favourite TV programmes.

www.evemag.com is an e-zine for teens.

Problem pages

www.adolescentadulthood.com is a fresh and fun problem site for all your relationship issues, including a dumpomatic break-up speech generator, for when you're having trouble ditching a bad boyfriend!

www.breakupgirl.com will help you through the difficult times, if you're newly-single and feeling at a loss.

www.thesite.org has help for every area of your life, with useful, unbiased information on everything from careers to drugs.

www.youth2youth.co.uk has links to a live e-mail and telephone helpline when you need instant help.

www.lifebyte.com offers advice on life's essentials, backed up by a bank of experts.

Educational resources

www.gcse.com to get help with GCSE level difficulties.

www.a-levels.co.uk is an A-Level portal, with educational links and online shopping for text books.

www.ucas.ac.uk is invaluable for anyone thinking about going to university, with full listings of courses and universities, advice and even online applications!

www.push.co.uk will give you the real advice on which university to choose, based on students' own experiences.

www.gapyear.com has everything you need to plan and find a successful gap year, whatever you end up doing with it.

www.homeworkhigh.com where you can get your difficult homework questions answered by real teachers!

www.homeworkelephant.co.uk is another great homework aid.
www.learn.co.uk from The Guardian, has all the educational resources you need at exam time.

For more education sites, see the full listings at the end of the *Education Online* chapter.

Payment cards

www.uksmart.co.uk lets you register to get a card, leaving you free to spend your Smartcreds at selected online stores.
www.rools.com get a rools prepay account and access exclusive deals from top online stores.
www.splashplastic.com lets you convert your cash into splashplastic money and shop online anywhere.
www.greenpeasoup.com pay in your cash at a top-up terminal to enjoy unlimited shopping on the net.

Music sites

www.napster.com is one of the most popular sites on the internet, letting you download software and MP3 music files from the internet.
www.worldpop.com has all the latest pop news, and details of the official UK and global charts.
www.audiostreet.com is one of the most popular and cheap music shopping sites on the net.
www.nme.com is a comprehensive site for anything musically alternative.
www.music.com is a US site for all tastes to get information on tours and latest releases.
www.pollstar.com lets you look up concert details for every act currently touring.
www.ticketmaster.co.uk – buy tickets for a huge number of events, without having to listen to hold music!
www.ejay.co.uk is a net radio station, where you can even compose your own electronic music!

Chapter 19

Silver Surfers

The UK is growing older gracefully, with the average age of the population increasing. In the next 20 years, half the adult population of Europe will be over the age of 45 and the phenomenal growth of this age group is mirrored online: the over-45s are the fastest growing demographic on the internet.

The image of the internet may be filled with trendy young things – but the real picture is that lots of mature consumers are spending time online. The internet is opening up a whole new world to older women. It provides them with a way of retaining their independence by enabling them to communicate quickly and easily with other people and organisations, as well as stimulating their minds and broadening their horizons.

The good news is that even as we get older we are refusing to act our age! With our stay young at heart attitude, the net is helping us hold on to youth. With a high disposable income and more spare time than most, the internet offers over 50s more choices and ways to make the most of this well-earned freedom.

Web Life – Silver surfers online

- Communicate instantly with family and friends all over the world via e-mail and instant messaging
- Research your hobbies and develop new interests, at **www.about.com**
- Shop for groceries, books, music or clothes online
- Buy a car online. Mintel research shows 30% of those aged over 50 buy cars
- Get help tracing your family tree by visiting genealogy websites like **www.familysearch.com** and **www.surnameweb.org**
- Look up long-lost friends from around the world, at **http://people.yahoo.com**
- Find out all about campaigning issues and make your voice heard, at **www.arp.org.uk**

A major issue for the older generation is lack of knowledge and confidence when it comes to the internet and computers in general. But there are many companies set up specifically to offer internet training. Take a look at **www.learnthenet.com** to find out more. Or get hold of the prospectus from your local College of Further Education, as most now run basic courses specifically aimed at those aged 55 plus.

Access to the internet is becoming less of a problem, as home computers become more affordable, cybercafes are appearing on every high street, and computer alternatives such as internet TV become more available.

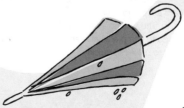

There is even a search engine especially focusing on older-interest sites! Go to **www.seniorsearch.com** and see what you can find!

Case study
Phyllis Butterfield

Phyllis Butterfield, aged 71, has not looked back since taking the plunge into the net: "I started using the internet last October. At first, I had not the faintest idea of how to use a computer, and thought I was too old to learn. I took a course which suited me perfectly, called Computing for the Terrified – believe me, at first I really was terrified, but I persevered nonetheless. Now I am thoroughly enjoying the internet experience – going online nearly every evening and at weekends. I may not be quite as up-to-speed as a younger person with more computer experience, but I'm getting there! I only wish computers had been around when I was younger."

One of the most popular sites for the over-45s is **www.vavo.com**, which enjoys great success due to the fact that it doesn't cater to the stereotypical version of the older generation. Its founder, Richard Spinks, is well aware of this age-old problem: "Older internet users appear to have similar requirements to most adults. They are no different in that they want (free!) access to comprehensive and relevant information and services delivered quickly".

Hobbies and interests

One of the great things about the net is that it provides an easy way to expand your horizons and interests. Many people take up hobbies on retirement; using the internet can be the ideal way to find a new hobby, or expand your interest in it. The best place to start is **www.about.com**, which has information on every possible interest, along with chat, forums and articles.

Case study
Paula Paul

Paula Paul from Datchet, Berkshire has been using the internet to pursue her interest in genealogy. She says: "I have been tracing my family tree via the internet and have made some interesting discoveries. I use a site called **www.genforum.genealogy.com** which lists enquiries by others interested in the same surnames. The Mormon Church has also made many old parish records available online for baptisms and marriages, on **www.familysearch.com**. Many genealogy groups are publishing their data online and although it is advisable to double-check the data, you can find cemetery records, lists of transportees and even replicas of actual documents. I was recently invited to a family reunion in Australia – the relevant ancestor was born in the East End of London". You can find an extensive list of genealogy websites at **www.cyndislist.com**.

You know it's time to log on when:

- You want to keep active and need to develop new interests
- You're interested in tracing your family history
- You don't have a clue about computers, but are still willing to try new things

Silver surfing sites

General resources

www.arp.org.uk, is the official site of the Association of Retired and Persons over 50, which has over 100,000 members and is known for its political activism on behalf of the older generation.
www.ageconcern.co.uk is a website for the UK charity, which explores issues and raises awareness, with plenty of information for those involved with caring for the very elderly. Also helpful is **www.helptheaged.org.uk**.
www.idf50.co.uk ('I don't feel 50!') for the funny and forthright opinions and contributions from its participating members.
www.theoldie.co.uk, is the online version of Richard Ingrams' incorrigible magazine for fogeys.
www.lifebegins.net is a glossy online magazine for women aged 50 plus, with advice from the Green Goddess, articles and competitions.
www.u3a.org.uk, the site of the University of the Third Age, which encourages people to continue learning after retirement. The site carries details of courses, links and other useful information.
www.saga.co.uk is the website of Saga holidays, who specialise in older-interest holidays.

Silver surfers portals

www.vienetwork.com is a very good starting-point, a UK site aimed at the over-50s focusing on leisure pursuits, money matters and body and mind. It has enough links for you to find your feet on the internet quickly and easily.

www.vavo.com is another portal for silver surfers, one which avoids the usual stereotypes, particularly strong on consumer issues. Eight million people have visited the Vavo site since its launch and use the site for a variety of reasons. It is the first and largest portal in Europe aimed at this age group.

www.seniority.co.uk is an online community for the over-50s which relies on its members' contributions, as well as lively discussion groups.

www.60-plus.co.uk is an independent site with a useful list of links recommended by members.

www.thirdage.com is an American portal for the young-at-heart, with a vibrant community, chatrooms and discussion boards on every topic.

Family trees online

www.about.com has information and links to every possible interest and hobby, including genealogy sites. Log on for fresh ideas on how to spend your free time.

www.pro.gov.uk is the homepage of the Public Record Office, who are in the process of transferring all existing records to the internet.

www.familysearch.com is the biggest ancestry website on the net. Run by the Mormons, it has over 25 million UK records, easily searched from the homepage.

www.genforum.genealogy.com
www.cyndislist.com
www.familyhistory.com
www.familytreemaker.com
www.familytreesearcher.com
www.surnameweb.org

Chapter 20

At your leisure

Your free time is valuable, so head online and make the most of it. An entertaining source of new ideas, the internet has something to stimulate the senses, boost creativity and inspire everyone with its infinite number of sites on every conceivable interest.

Why not start relaxing by listening to the music of your choice direct from the net. Tune into one of the hundreds of internet-based radio stations out there. Try **www.internetradiolist.com** to find your favourite station. Most offer great sound quality even on a 56k modem. Or catch a concert online at The House of Blues, **www.hob.com**. **www.gmn.com** is the home of the Global Music Network, which has weekly webcasts of classical and jazz concerts from all over the world.

Then again you could always settle down with some chocolates and the latest best-seller, both bought online from **www.thorntons.co.uk** and **www.amazon.co.uk**, of course! Keep in touch with what's going on in the book world at sites like **www.bookerprize.co.uk** and **www.orangeprize.co.uk**, where you can find out what the hottest books are. **www.about.com** hosts great resources on women writers, so you can log on and discuss your favourites with other women.

Web Life – Time to spare?

* Become a culture vulture and check on the art scene online or visit one of the many exhibitions, museums or galleries on **www.24hourmuseum.org.uk**

* Learn to play a musical instrument, get your instrument, music sheets and tuition online at **www.musicscales.co.uk** and **www.abcmusic.co.uk**

* Discover the secrets of the heavens at **www.extremescience.com**

* Let those green fingers transform the garden, with advice from **www.garden.com** and **www.gardenworld.co.uk**

* Volunteer your skills to a good cause at **www.do-it.org.uk**

* Create your own website at **www.moonfruit.com**

* Find equestrian news, a new riding club, or a new horse or pony at **www.horseandhound.co.uk**, and **www.equine-world.co.uk**

* Become a movie buff at **www.imdb.com**

* Cook a gourmet meal with the best selection of organic ingredients **www.organicsdirect.com**

* Keep your furry friends happy with a new toy or accessory **www.pets-pyjamas.co.uk**

Cultural pursuits

From museums to theme parks there are hundreds of places away from your computer to keep you and your friends and family happy. And if you can't think of any, then head for **www.planit4kids.com** which has a handy list of local activities to keep you occupied. Venture into the art scene, by discovering museums and galleries that appeal to you.

Enjoy the arts? With the internet at your disposal, there's no more excuses about not having the time to read the latest reviews, or book tickets in time. Just head for **www.timeout.com**, which will bring you the latest clubs, arts, events, theatre in cities around the world. **www.whatsonstage.com** is the homepage of the National Performing Arts Information Service, an indispensable way to keep up to date with the theatre world and book tickets to the hottest shows.

Change your perceptions with a compelling insight into contemporary London, **www.ica.org.uk** is the home of the Institute of Contemporary Arts with online digital art, talks, films and more. Or visit the more traditional galleries like **www.tate.org.uk**, As you browse through the Tate's 11,000 images online you will be inspired to head for one of their amazing galleries across the country.

If you want to own your own art, head for one of the commercial online galleries. **www.art-connection.com** puts you in touch with London's top galleries, or try your hand at an online auction at **www.sothebys.com** and you may end up with your owning a masterpiece. **www.eyestorm.com** is a flourishing site selling modern art prints and photography from fashionable artists.

If you're a film buff, the internet has plenty to offer. Add some classics to your video/DVD collection and save time and money buying from **www.blackstar.co.uk**. This site has a much wider range of films than the high street, and lower prices too! If you need film inspiration the internet movie database at **www.imdb.com**, offers a massive array of facts on films, stars and trivia.

Food for thought

For food lovers, the internet offers the perfect recipe for success. Brush up your own culinary skills at **www.simplyfood.com** or **www.bbc.co.uk/foodanddrink**. Even the most hopeless cook will soon get the hang of cooking with all the online help available. However, if you're pushed for time but want to eat well, try **www.leapingsalmon.com**, who deliver easy meal kits to your home. All you have to do is pour yourself a glass of wine and get stirring.

Celebrity chefs are getting wired up, delivering their hot and steamy advice online. Take a trip to **www.jamieoliver.net**, **www.nigella.com** and **www.bbc.co.uk/food** and extend your culinary skills without having to spend a week at cookery school.

If you're a wine drinker, there's plenty to tempt your tastebuds on the net. Try **www.vine2wine.com**, a wine portal with hundreds of links. **www.jancisrobinson.com** is the homepage of The Financial Times wine correspondent. If you already know what you're looking for, try **www.winesearcher.com**.

The great outdoors

With a destination in mind, let **www.ordsvy.gov.uk** take your planning one step further by downloading a map to get you there on time. With leisure maps, historical plans, touring and rambling routes there is no excuse for getting lost ever again.

Brighten up your day with a little gardening. **www.crocus.co.uk** will soon get you outside planting a few bulbs. There are lots of tips to turn your fingers green, even if you start off not knowing weeds from tulips. You can also buy gardening supplies and plants. **www.bbc.co.uk/gardening** has the latest tips from Alan Titchmarsh to keep your garden at its best, no matter what the season. There's even a gardening site especially for women! Earth-mother types should log on to **www.yougrowgirl.com**.

Case Study
Cress Rolfe

"Having never had computer training at school, I was a computer novice until about six years ago. I had used computers at work, at a book publishers but my interest grew in the mid-nineties as I found out about the internet. I could see that the net was a much more immediate and empowering way to get information published. I started programming web pages myself in HTML, learning from books and evening classes.

"I have played lacrosse for the English national team, as well as on local and regional levels. Many women's sports suffer from lack of publicity – which is why I decided to launch my own site on the subject. **www.sportsfix.co.uk** aims to gain more publicity for women's sports and encourage women to participate and watch a range of sports, from netball and lacrosse, to martial arts and aerobics. The strength of the site is that, as well as finding out about what's going on in their area, women can post details of their own events on the site for free, by entering the information into an online form. Access to publishing their own information like this is empowering for teams and individuals, and the site should raise the profile of all women's sport by listing it all together in one place.

"I produced the site by myself, in my spare time. I was able to fund it with a Millennium Award grant from the Peabody Trust (**www.peabody.org.uk**) who are a London-based charitable trust, and I got help creating the database from **www.ethicalmedia.com**, a web-design company who work with the charity sector. The success of **www.sportsfix.co.uk** will depend on the participation of its visitors – eventually I'm hoping it will become a vehicle for encouraging more women to take part in all kinds of sport."

Pet pampering

What better way to relax than pampering your favourite friend?
www.petspark.com has special toys for your pets, like a fantastic
range of accessories to keep them warm and entertained. With
lots of cute pictures and stories, sites like **www.puppies.co.uk**
and **www.animail.co.uk** keep kids happy for hours, but could
lead to a new furry or feathered friend joining the family!

Before you become a pet owner, it's worth getting advice.
www.rspca.org is the home of the RSPCA, with information on looking
after all kinds of animals. **www.dogshome.org** puts you in touch with
the famous Battersea Dogs home. **www.horseandhound.co.uk** has
information on looking after horses and will help you pick the right one.

Whatever your passion, whatever your scene, you're sure to find some
inspiration online. Unearth the truth about the stars, get a review of the
latest film, snowboarding and gardening tips. Leisure sites are diverse
as the many ways people spend their time. So reach for the mouse,
however obscure your interests, there are bound to be sites with new
gear, new reviews, new angles, new facts.

You know it's time to log on when:

* The last hobby you had was learning french at school
* You want to change the scenery inside and out
* The only art you've seen for years is pinned to the fridge

Leisure sites

Film sites

www.imdb.co.uk is the Internet Movie Database.
www.popcorn.co.uk has listings for all films showing in the UK.
www.filmsunlimited.co.uk is The Guardian's film site.
www.radiotimes.com/film

The Arts

www.artnet.com
www.artstar.com
www.24hourmuseum.org.uk is an online database of museums from all over the UK.
www.nmwa.org is the homepage of the American National Museum of Women in the Arts.
www.artguide.org is an easy way to find your favourite paintings.
www.art-connection.com is an online directory of London's commercial galleries.
www.nationalgallery.org.uk is the homepage of the National Gallery.
www.royalacademy.org.uk
www.sothebys.com run online art, antique and jewellery auctions.
www.christies.com has online and offline Arts auctions.
www.eyestorm.com sells contemporary prints.
www.artrepublic.com is an art portal which also sells prints.
www.artefact.co.uk is a monthly art magazine.
www.bl.uk is the homepage of the British Library.
www.ica.org.uk is the ICA.
www.tate.org.uk for the Tate Gallery.

Pet sites

www.thepetcenter.com will fulfil all your pet's needs.
www.petspark.com is a pet superstore online.
www.petspyjamas.co.uk for online pet supplies.
www.animalnet.com has a directory of animal clubs and breeders.
www.petforkids.co.uk for pet shopping on the net.

Cooking

www.simplyfood.com is Carlton TV's food network.
www.bbc.co.uk/foodanddrink is the homepage of Food and Drink, with Jilly Goolden.
www.therepertoire.com is a culinary workstation to help you with your cooking difficulties.
www.my-meals.com lets you create your own meals online.
www.leapingsalmon.com will deliver you a kit to make your own, delicious, home-cooked meal.
www.jamieoliver.net
www.nigella.com is Nigella Lawson's homepage.
www.ichef.com is an American site with over 30,000 recipes.

Gardening

www.bbc.co.uk/gardening is the home of Charlie Dimmock and Alan Titchmarsh.
www.gardenersworld.beeb.com is the BBC's gardening-themed chat site.
www.rhs.org.uk is the homepage of the Royal Horticultural Society.
www.crocus.co.ukwww.gardenworld.co.uk
www.garden-uk.org.uk

Chapter 21

Health and Fitness on the Net

Save your excuses, with one click you can feel better than ever, courtesy of the internet. Log on for thousands of health hints and tips. A combination of the world's biggest medical library and the ultimate 'support group', the net should be the first port of call for people wanting to improve their wellbeing.

If you want to know more about a particular condition, you can look up a range of medical journals online. If you're worried you might have something, you can visit a virtual doctor or try one of the diagnostic systems available. If you're interested in alternative or complementary therapies, you can get information even if your GP is sceptical. If you need motivation to get fit, you can join in with 'live' exercise classes. If you want to give up smoking, you can get the inspiration and step-by-step support you need. And if you want to network with other sufferers, you'll find forums on every condition, from the everyday to the extremely rare. So there's no need to worry that you might have something serious, or forget about healthy eating because you don't know what to cook – whatever you need to know, you'll find it on the internet.

Case Study
Colette Ware

"A year ago my son was diagnosed with coeliac disease, which I had never heard of. I went to the internet to find out more about this disease and now I'm a lot more knowledgeable. I've learnt about everything from treatments to causes. I even get sent medical updates – information which would be difficult to find in other ways."

Tip

Find out about giving up smoking at
www.ash.org.uk

Doctors on the net

If you have a question about your health, you can get it answered by a qualified doctor, online, in a matter of minutes and around the clock, through a variety of internet medical services. Easy and quick to use, these services are ideal for minor ailments that it's not worth going to your own GP for. Of course, if it might be more serious – and if the online service advises it – see your doctor without delay! **www.nhsdirect.nhs.uk** has round-the-clock help via a hotline staffed by nurses, as well as advice on treating minor symptoms yourself. **www.netdoctor.co.uk** has good self-treatment advice and diagnostic tools that check your symptoms against a range of conditions. **www.e-med.co.uk** – 'your doctor, wherever you go' will even give you a consultation with your personal physician via e-mail or webcam!

Women's health sites

It might be an idea to look at sites focusing on women's health. These sites have information on everything relating to women's health issues, from dieting to pregnancy to the menopause. Most of the women's portals contain health channels as well, so there's plenty out there for women. Try **www.handbag.com/health**, or more specialised sites like **www.womens-health.com**.

Online health and fitness

If you're in good health and want to stay that way – or if you want to shape up and get fit, the internet's right behind you. There are sites to help you with fitness and training, diets and workout schedules, and nutrition sites to make sure you're eating right. A great place to start is **www.active.org.uk**. After a visit, you'll be convinced of the benefits of healthier living and keen to get started straight away.

Perhaps you, like most of us, would like to be fitter too but you don't know where to start? Check out **www.atozfitness.com**. With over 1,000 links to a complete range of health and fitness-related sites – you're bound to find some ideas. **www.health-club.net** has a comprehensive list of health, sport, leisure clubs in your local area, searchable by postcode. Or if you're interested in a particular sport or activity, you'll find thousands of choices online.

www.runnersworld.ltd.uk, for example, will help you out, whether you want to train for the marathon or just take a quick run around the block. It will even help you find the perfect running shoes.
If you'd like to beat stress without sweat, increase your flexibility and improve your posture, activities such as yoga or Tai Chi could be for you. Take a look at **www.yogasite.com** for inspiration.

Diet and nutrition on the net

Eating a nutritious, wholesome diet is probably one of the most important investments you can make in your health. If you think you could do with losing a few pounds, you can learn about delicious, yet healthy eating at **www.cyberdiet.com**. They'll even e-mail you encouraging messages to keep you inspired.

With new developments coming along all the time and constant scare stories in the media, it can be difficult to sort the hype from the facts about what's safe to eat and what to avoid. You'll find the whole picture at sites like **www.mynutrition.com,** which includes a section on food allergies. If you'd not only prefer your fruit and vegetables to be naturally produced but would also like them delivered straight to your door, try the service offered by **www.organicsdirect.com**.

Web Life – Healthy surfing

- Find out about the power of plants and natural medicine on the homeopathy site **www.drlockie.com**
- Give yourself a virtual makeover and discover a new you, at **www.changeslive.com**
- Take a natural approach to health and nutrition at **www.thinknatural.com**
- Choose a beauty salon or health spa from the directory at **www.britishservices.co.uk**

Case study
Stella Lewington, 54

"I've always been naturally fit and healthy, with a zest for living. As my body weight and size have remained constant throughout my adulthood, I've never felt the need to join a gym or concentrate on exercise. But one memorable and certainly painful day for me changed this feeling, after competing in the London Marathon for charity. I wish I could have found out about the benefits of exercise beforehand and avoided those sore muscles and blistered feet!

"Websites like **www.drkoop.com** provide me with up to date information on how to deal with problems as small as a minor blister to serious illnesses. All of the information can be found easily and is laid out in simple terms – and there's no queuing to see the GP.

"Prior to joining my local gym I wanted to learn about the correct way to exercise. I have always enjoyed reading health books, but knew that the best information for me would be on the internet, because it would be the most up to date. Since then, **www.netfit.co.uk** has become my fitness guidebook, giving me both knowledge and confidence – it's like having an online personal trainer."

Looking good and beating stress

As everyone who leads a busy life will know, relaxation and pampering are an essential part of beating potentially fatal stress. If you'd like to take a different approach to wellbeing and lead a more harmonious life, try **www.absolutehealth.co.uk** which concentrates on alternative therapies like Alexander Technique and offers DIY kits for you to use at home. **www.acupuncture.com** will teach you everything you need to know about acupuncture therapy.

www.sleepcouncil.org.uk is the home of the Sleep Council, with tips on getting a good night's sleep and a range of alternative products such as aromatherapy. If you want to change your look as well as your body, try **www.changeslive.com.** This interactive site lets you try out new hairstyles and makeup online, so you can check out new styles before you take the plunge.

You know it's time to log on when:

- Your clothes seem to have shrunk...
- A friend has been diagnosed with an illness and you want to find out more
- You can't seem to get rid of your cold, but don't want the hassle of going to the doctor

---

Health websites

General health sites

http://news.bbc.co.uk/education/health has all the latest on health research and other health-related news. Or try **www.reutershealth.com**. **www.healthfinder.com** is a medical search engine – the perfect jumping-off point.
www.hospitalweb.co.uk is a large UK health portal, or try **www.ukhealthnet.co.uk**.
www.embarrassingproblems.co.uk is the place to go if you have a sensitive problem you don't want to share with your doctor.

www.allcures.com is an online health library with a pharmacy attached. It's a good place to find out more about your medication.

www.mediconsult.com is a community site for all kinds of diseases, where you can interact with other sufferers on bulletin boards and get support.

www.graylab.ac.uk/omd is an online medical dictionary, so that you can look up any medical jargon you don't understand.

www.kidshealth.org is an American site focusing on kids' health problems.

www.healthatoz.com is a complete health portal and can be personalised to suit you.

www.healthinfocus.co.uk is a big information site focusing on treatments available on the NHS. Similarly, try **www.healthgate.co.uk**.

www.personal-screening.com is a health site concentrating on illness prevention – and you can test yourself for common illnesses.

www.ivanhoe.com has updates on the latest medical advances.

www.wddty.co.uk is an eye-opening site telling you 'what doctors don't tell you'.

Women's health sites

www.womens-health.com find out about the most common women's health problems; chat to other members about your condition.

www.icircle.com/health is the health channel from the icircle women's portal.

www.fpa.org.uk is the homepage of the Family Planning Association.

www.healthsquare.com is for women and families with general health tips.

www.healthyideas.com is a women's fitness site.

www.women.com is an American portal with a good health section.

www.ivillage.co.uk diet and fitness.

www.handbag.com/health.

www.lovelife.uk.com is a sexual health site aimed at young women.

www.gyn101.com and **www.obgyn.net** are American gynaecological sites.

Doctors on the net

www.nhsdirect.nhs.uk is part of the NHS's at-home treatment programme for minor ailments like colds. It has a wide range of articles and links, and you can also call their helpline if you can't find what you're looking for.

www.drkoop.com. This well-known US webdoctor has all the latest health news, a comprehensive encyclopaedia and a women's health channel.

www.drweil.com is an alternative medical practitioner, online.

www.drlockie.com is your own personal homeopath, on the net!

www.netdoctor.co.uk is an independent health site run by British GPs, with plenty of info and regular chat sessions.

www.patient.co.uk is a British health directory, with links to your local healthcare providers.

www.e-med.co.uk provides a way to manage your healthcare over the net, by interacting with real doctors using e-mail and webcams. Perfect for avoiding that busy waiting room!

www.2psych.com is an e-mail counselling site. Receive one-to-one help from your computer.

www.docnet.org.uk is a community site for doctors that's still useful for patients.

www.24dr.com is the home of the 24 hour doctor – just ask the doctor a question, and wait for a fast reply.

Fitness sites

www.netfit.co.uk

www.atozfitness.com

www.health-club.net has a directory of UK gyms and workout facilities, so you can look up a gym in your area!

www.fitnesslink.com is a peppy American workout site with plenty of ideas.

www.active.org.uk is the Government's site to encourage us all to become more active.

www.yogasite.com focuses on the health craze of the moment, yoga.

www.runnersworld.com, **www.newrunner.com** and
www.womensrunning.com will help you if you're planning to take up
jogging your way to health.
www.bodydoctorfitness.com is the page of the personal trainer to the
stars David Marshall, who gives tips on toning up and losing weight.

Diets and nutrition

www.cyberdiet.com
www.medicinecabinet.co.uk is a UK site to help you boost your
nutrition and fitness levels.
www.healthcalc.net will help you work out the healthiest ways of
eating for you.
www.mynutrition.co.uk to find out about nutrition, vitamins and
eating well.
www.weightwatchers.com has all you need to know about the weight
watchers diet and to find your nearest meeting.
www.feelingfat.net is an online guide to losing weight through
healthy eating.

Health alternatives

www.absolutehealth.co.uk focuses on natural cures and
alternative medicine.
www.stressrelease.com
http://altmedicine.about.com is about.com's great site on
alternative medicine.
www.alternativemedicine.com to find out about the latest
alternative therapies.
www.alexandertechnique.com
www.nelsonbach.com/bachessessnces for Flower Remedies.
www.acupuncture.org for the British Acupuncture Council.
www.chiropractic-uk.co.uk is the British Chiropractic Association.
www.hom-inform.org is the British Homeopathic Library.

Health spas and treatments

www.britishservices.co.uk/beautysalons.htm has a good directory of UK health farms.

www.healthclubs.org.uk has an online directory of local gyms.

Specific illnesses

www.crc.org.uk is the homepage of the Cancer Research Campaign, with updates on the latest research.

www.mhsource.com is Mental Health InfoSource, a site focusing on informing you about mental health issues, including chatrooms and a guide to different treatments and therapies.

www.avert.com is an AIDS education site.

www.alcoholics-anonymous.org

www.alzheimers.org.uk

www.tht.org.uk is the homepage of the Terence Higgins Trust AIDS charity.

www.bcc-uk.org is the Breast Cancer Campaign.

www.scope.org for the cerebral palsy charity, Scope.

www.ash.org.uk is a site to help you give up smoking.

www.allergy-info.com has everything you need to know about all allergies.

www.aanma.org is the allergy and asthma network.

www.cardiac.org.uk is the British Cardiac Society.

www.epilepsy.org.uk

www.disabilitynow.org.uk

www.dsa-uk.com is the Down's Syndrome Association.

www.mencap.org.uk

www.mind.org.uk

www.mssociety.org.uk: the Multiple Sclerosis Society.

www.pms.org.uk is the National Association for Pre-menstrual Syndrome.

Health and fitness products online

www.iris-online.co.uk offers quick and cheap delivery on a wide range of contact lenses.

www.allcures.com is the UK's first online chemist.

www.pharmacy2u.co.uk

www.boots.co.uk is the website of the high street giant, with e-commerce and information.

www.superdrug.co.uk

www.holistichands.co.uk sells cruelty-free and natural beauty and therapy products.

www.changeslive.com is a fun way to give yourself a virtual makeover.

www.sweatybetty.com has a great range of attractive workout wear for women. See also **www.sweatshop.co.uk**.

www.zipvit.co.uk sells discounted vitamins.

Chapter 22

Love Bytes

As the internet is becoming an increasingly important part of our personal lives, it can even fill those lonely nights with warm, rewarding communications, opening up conversations and relationships with people around the world.

Forget blind date nerves, inane chat in smoky pubs or crowded clubs, if you're looking for fun, excitement, romance or even marriage, the internet is a great place to play the dating game. With over 11 million singles in the UK at the last count and less and less leisure time to spend finding Mr Right, there's a wealth of possibilities online.

Just like at any party or social event, you have the chance to mix with a real cross section of people, from the charming to the boring. You can visit chatrooms and listen to the conversations and get to know the community. On dating sites, you can check out the cleverly designed application forms and decide for yourself whether the personal descriptions are really true...

It's anonymous – you can be whoever you want, even someone completely new. But beware that this can work both ways. Your dreamy six foot hunk may turn out to be a weedy five footer!

It's safe – as long as you stick to a few simple guidelines, you can have all sorts of erotic pleasures without the risks of the real world.

And it's exciting – if you're looking for fun, the net can make you feel like a teenager again. In a way, the internet brings back the joys of old fashioned romance. You can delay physical contact and enjoy the power of words – of flirting, of getting to know each other and making friends before making love.

For many people, the internet has become a place to come to terms with their sexual orientation, explore their identity, share fantasies, sort out relationship problems and search for potential partners from a 'bank' of millions.

Divorce Online

In contrast to the dating opportunities offered online, the internet has also made it easier to obtain a divorce! The new divorce sites offer cheaper, quicker divorces, as well as more information about getting divorced. If you're thinking of making a clean break of it, log on to **www.divorce-online.co.uk**, **www.quickedivorce.co.uk** and **www.divorce.uk.com** to solve your marital problems.

Case Study
Su Newman

Meet, fall in love and get married on the internet. Isn't it a media fantasy? Step up Su Newman who met Paul in December 1999, exchanged e-mails, spent Christmas together, got engaged in January and married in May 2000. Both previously married, Paul, 41, and Su, 35, joined and met thanks to Club Sirius, **www.clubsirius.com** a UK-based introduction agency with a membership running into many thousands.

Comments Su: "I joined Sirius in summer of 1999 and used their website to read profiles of men looking for sensible, long-term relationships. I read Paul's in December and we immediately began exchanging e-mails. I liked his sense of humour and attitude to life. After we'd meet for an evening out we'd then go home and exchange e-mails late into the night!" Of course, they discovered that they lived only seven miles from each other in the Surrey countryside, but if it hadn't been for Sirius they might as well have been living on opposite sides of the globe.

Did Paul propose on the net? Not quite – but close. Mainly thanks to their professions – Su is an engineering accountant and Paul is an international sales manager – they are both internet experts. Says Su: "We also used **www.lastminute.com** to find a hotel for the proposal. Paul wanted to propose to me with bags of style so we made it a 'Proposal Weekend' at a fabulous hotel and then decided to use the same hotel for the marriage ceremony and wedding reception!" The net involvement didn't stop there. Now at home, looking after her children as well as husband Paul, Su is a big champion of the internet – "I knew how valuable the internet was as a business tool," says Su. "But I'd never really appreciated how powerful a tool it could be in my personal life until I joined Sirius and discovered that I could visit their site at any time, even two in the morning, to read profiles, and get human backup as well."

Modern matchmaking

Looking for Mr Right has never been easy, but you'll be amazed at how the internet can help you find that perfect partner. There's no need to join a gym, or eye up the office talent, just log on to one of the many dating sites that offer services to suit every taste. And when you find the man of your dreams, you can use technology to play the right dating games.

If you want some fun playing roles and trying out different erotic identities, check out **www.virtuallydating.com**. Here, you can create a virtual cartoon of yourself, from your clothes and hair colour to your personality, depending on your mood. There are chatrooms, horoscopes and agony aunts too.

Elite, gorgeous, successful twenty somethings should try **www.gorgeousgettogethers.com** and arrange to go on a hot date with lots of men in one night. Dating and chat sites offer safety in numbers and encourage you to stick to the golden rules of online dating: always meet in public places, and let others know where you are.

For those looking for more serious commitment, try out one of the sites promising lifelong partnerships, marriage and that special happiness only a loving relationship can bring. The American site **www.bematched.com** claims to have been instrumental in thousands of marriages and is now bringing the same dream to the UK. With photographs of potential partners and an easy to search format, it's serious if you are!

If you really want to find Mr Right, he may not come free. Most of the more professional online dating agencies charge a subscription fee of up to £40 a month, depending on the service. But they do offer added benefits such as online chatrooms and a more up-to-date database than traditional agencies. Try **www.dateline.co.uk** or **www.clubsirius.com** to find your perfect match.

Being careful

The media is keen to hype up the idea that the internet is a hotbed of everything from paedophilia to violence. But, while the erotic and unsavoury side of the internet does exist, just like in the real world, intimate sexual content and pornography makes up less than 1% of internet. It is easily possible to keep clear of those places you don't want to visit, simply leave a site if it doesn't appeal.

Hot Tips

If you are interacting with strangers online, there are a few safety tips to bear in mind:

- Be careful – remember people may not be what they seem or what they claim, so never give your home address and phone number, no matter how well you hit it off
- Go public – if you hit it off with someone, you will inevitably want to get together. If you do, meet up in a public place, preferably accompanied by a friend and let someone know where you are and when you will be back. Basically, take no risks
- Say 'no' to harassment – even initially pleasant encounters can turn nasty. If you experience any online harassment, remember it can get worse, so give no encouragement. If you receive messages that offend, politely say you are not interested and stop communication
- Use your instincts. If something doesn't seem right, don't give it the benefit of the doubt
- Look up more dating safety tips on **www.wildxangel.com**

See the *Surfing Safely* chapter for more tips on staying safe when you're online.

Case Study
Anita Nowinska

Not everyone finds love at the click of a mouse. Anita thinks finding love online is as likely as winning the lottery, especially given the difficulty of gauging chemistry online.

"About a year ago I started this online adventure, internet dating. I'm a 35 year-old businesswoman, the classic intimidating creature men find difficult to deal with. So I started to use the net and have spoken to more people than you can imagine. I've met so many men that I've now got my own rating system!

"Firstly there are the complete perverts, whose e-mails would shame the porn channels. The romantic charmer is also easy to find – they are after the same thing as the perverts but just manage to be a little more subtle about it. A small percentage of desirable good looking men can be found, but with them you have to compete with the image of the perfect goddess they are convinced they will find online.

"It certainly livens up your day, like meeting the guy that used to be a woman, or the six foot stunner who ends up being a five foot wimp. Not forgetting the men that fall in love instantly after one date and want you to have their babies! **www.udate.com** and **www.datingdirect.com** have a really active membership and are easy to use. Datingdirect does filter out the abusive e-mails, but on udate you might be in for some surprisingly candid messages!

"There are a lot of desperate people out there, so you need to be careful where and who you meet. For me it's been like doing the lottery, light hearted fun with little chance of winning the jackpot. If you have your heart set on meeting your soul mate you may be disappointed, there are great people out there, don't take it too seriously, and have some fun – it's pure entertainment."

You're not a loser if you log on to find love. It gives both freedom and choice and the opportunity to get to know each other slowly over seductive e-mail. And even if there is no chemistry when you meet in the real world, at least you're out and having fun.

> ### You know it's time to log on when:
>
> - You have been dumped by your longtime lover
> - You're looking for old fashioned flirting and romance
> - You want some fun but don't want to go out to find it

Net romance

Dating sites

www.virtuallydating.com is a funky new site offering role playing, a games lounge and chat rooms.

www.match.com is the biggest US online dating service.

www.love-makers.com lets you browse personal ads, or place your own.

www.one-and-only.com helps you meet men from all over the world, using all kinds of criteria to narrow down your search.

www.venusdating.co.uk is a UK-based payment site, with its own instant messaging system.

www.dating.co.uk gives you access to free personal ads and photos.

www.flirt.com – this portal has over 500,000 members, giving you a chance to connect to people with similar interests, using personal ads, advice forums and chatting.

www.gorgeousgettogethers.com if you're too busy to date, try speed dating. Get matched up with four guaranteed-gorgeous blind dates in one night!

www.bematched.com – a free UK dating site for 18-30 year olds, with global access for a wider range of potential partners.

www.dateline.co.uk – take a free computer test from the longest-established dating agency in the UK, with a telephone helpline if you have any problems.

www.clubsirius.com – this site runs events and even holidays for single, well-educated and articulate people.

www.culturelovers.com will help you find a lover who loves the Arts.

www.onlylunch.co.uk will organise lunch dates so you can find love in the daytime.

www.natural-friends.com will enable you to meet other spiritually aware people.

www.gliagency.co.uk is a large Gay and Lesbian, non-scene agency.

www.countrypartners.co.uk is especially for people who live in rural areas, or who enjoy country pursuits.

www.friendfinder.com is a site with over 3,000 UK members.

www.nomorefrogs.com uses psychometric testing so you can find out exactly what someone is like.

www.woowho.co.uk is a hip dating site to help you boost your social life.

www.totallyjewish.com specialises in finding you a Jewish partner.

Romance sites

www.hullucinations.com/dearlynda is where Lynda will answer your e-mails with help and advice on your internet dating problems.

www.lovestory.com.au: read others' eye-opening internet love stories from all over the world.

www.swoon.com has horoscopes and advice to help you on your path to true love.

www.secretadmirer.com. Find out if your secret passion is requited, by sending the object of your affection an anonymous e-mail. If they reply, you've met your match!

www.loveisgreat.com is the home page of love. If you're feeling slushy, this site has everything romance-related.

www.inspirationpoint.com is a complete romance resource, helping you to keep a spark in your relationship.

www.1001waystoberomantic will help you keep the spark of passion going.

www.cyber-loving.com has advice especially for online relationships.

www.rom101.com take compatibility tests online and find out if your love was meant to be.

Erotica

www.sexilicious.com is a women's forum for an open and frank discussion of sexuality and sexual issues.

www.scarletletters.com is a journal of erotica for women.

Romantic gifts and flowers

www.interflora.co.uk will help you say it with flowers.

www.flowersbydirect.co.uk has next day delivery for the whole UK for flowers.

www.giftstore.co.uk will send a selection of flowers, cards and gifts anywhere.

www.giftdelivery.co.uk has a romantic selection of gifts.

Chapter 23

Travel Easy

The internet could almost have been invented for travellers. Whether you're looking for a cheap family package, planning a six month backpacking trip, checking the weather at your destination or need to stay in touch while you're away, the net's the place to be. Women are usually responsible for booking family holidays, so it's worth seeing what's available online.

First of all, the net can help you decide where to go. You'll find a vast amount of information on any destination you could possibly imagine, from online guidebooks like **www.lonelyplanet.com**, to official resort websites, like **www.disneyworld.com**. Just do a search on the country, the region, even the resort itself, if you know it, and you'll be amazed at what you find.

When you've chosen your destination, you can be fully prepared before you leave – from packing the right clothes to learning a few useful phrases and checking the exchange rate at the currency converter **www.xe.net/ucc/**. It's much more fun – and more convenient – than dealing with travel agents and tourist offices, especially if departure is imminent! Once you've decided where to go, and where to stay, you can often book and pay online – sorting out your whole holiday with nothing more than a mouse.

Another advantage of arranging your holidays via the internet is that it's instant. If you like to do things spontaneously, you can pick up some excellent deals at the drop of a hat from sites like **www.lastminute.com**. And because you can organise everything, from hotels to car hire, in minutes, you can act on impulse and still enjoy a high quality of service. Holiday operators often dump their unsold capacity on the net at very low prices – so being impulsive always pays off.

Women travellers

There are good resources for women travellers to be found on the net. It's really useful to be able to keep in touch with friends and family via e-mail while you are travelling, especially if you're going it alone. **www.vagabunda.com** is a fun travelling site for women, focusing on real life travelling stories. It has great safety tips, and you can also look up a country's customs: worth knowing if you want to avoid undue hassle as you travel!

Hot Tips – Travel online

- If you want to 'picture' your destination, check out the internet webcams at **www.i-spy.com**
- Chat to others, get travel tips and insider knowledge of where you're going, at **www.lonelyplanet.com**
- If you need cash, find your nearest cashpoint at **www.visa.com** or **www.mastercard.com**
- Find out about any local difficulties from the Foreign Office's site at **www.fco.gov.uk/travel**
- Get maps for anywhere in the world at **www.mapquest.com**
- Go to any tourist office in the world, look it up at **www.towd.com**
- If you want to name your own price for flights, accommodation and car hire, try **www.priceline.com**

Travelling light

The internet is a haven for the budget traveller, especially when it comes to cheap flights. There is always a great selection of good value deals, especially if you're prepared to be flexible about your departure dates and times. So, instead of phoning round for hours, try heading for one of the budget travel sites like **www.statravel.com** and see what's available.

Sloping off

The search for that elusive commodity 'snow', has just been made easier. Now, thanks to **www.snow-forecast.com** you can be e-mailed with the latest snow situation in over 300 resorts around the world, for a small fee. All you need to do then is phone a few friends and book your holiday.

Web Life – Travel resources

* Bargain flights – try **www.buzzaway.com, www.go-fly.com, www.easyjet.com**, **www.ryanair.com**, **www.britishairways.com** and **www.expedia.co.uk**

* Early bird discounts – many tour operators offer you up to 15% discount if you book early, check out **www.thomson-holidays.com** or **www.virginholidays.com**

* Special late deals can save hundreds of pounds and are available on most travel sites. Start with **www.lastminute.com**

* If you want a better deal on your travel insurance **www.egg.com** has some great offers for all the family

* Online travel guides – see what's going on before you get there at **www.roughguides.com**, covering everything from where to eat, stay, transport and visa requirements

* Basic translation services are available online at **www.babelfish.altavista.com** and **http://translator.go.com** giving you the choice phrases you need to make your holiday more enjoyable

* Holiday health problems needn't ruin your trip. Make sure you have all the necessary jabs and other precautions at **www.fitfortravel.scot.nhs.uk**

* Resort guides like **www.puertopollensa.com** are an invaluable way to find out about your destination.

Case study
Kate Adamson

"I have been a keen traveller since my Gap year, when I went to Nepal for twelve months to teach English a few years before the internet became really widespread. Before the internet, communicating with my family and friends at home was really difficult and expensive. I used to have to get faxes sent to me care of a hotel, but they often went missing.

"Now that the internet has made the world so much smaller, communicating while I am away is a breeze! I've never been to any country, no matter how remote, that didn't have some kind of cybercafe I could use. I've even sat in the middle of the South American rainforest and looked up what's going on at home on the BBC's news site, **www.bbc.co.uk/news**.

"I can e-mail my friends and family and let them know I'm OK, and get the crucial gossip from home – and it's so cheap and fast! I have a hotmail account, **www.hotmail.com**, so I can access my inbox from anywhere on the net. It's also incredibly useful to e-mail other friends who are travelling, to arrange where and when to meet up on the road.

"The other thing the internet has helped is for researching my trips. I use it before I go away to book cheap flights from **www.sta.com** and also while I'm away. There are so many travellers sites out there – I use the online guidebook at **www.lonelyplanet.com** and the Foreign Office's indispensable site at **www.fco.gov.uk**. I went around Asia by myself last summer, to countries like Laos, Vietnam and Cambodia. Before I went, and while I was travelling, I was able to check the political situation in each country – which really put my mind at rest!"

Adventures on the net

If you want a holiday with a difference, the internet helps you find much more than just cheap air fares and hotels. Safaris, white water rafting, cultural and eco-tours, cycling, mountaineering, expeditions to remote regions, ranching and scuba diving are just some of the experiences awaiting the intrepid traveller online. The internet has opened up a whole new world of holidays, both on and off the beaten track.

If you're looking for the trip of a lifetime, you no longer need a helpful travel agent prepared to do hours of work for you. The internet can put you in touch with the experts to help with everything from vaccinations to visas.

While you're away, you can still make the most of the internet, if you want to! If you have a webmail account, you can keep in touch, with friends, family, even the office. One of the most popular webmail providers is **www.hotmail.com.**

You know it's time to log on when:

- You're buried under a pile of uninspiring travel brochures
- You want an exotic holiday – at a budget price – at the last minute
- You need to get away from the office

Travel websites

General resources for travellers

www.fco.gov.uk/travel will have travel warnings and advice for
your destination, with information about terrorists and health risks
around the world.
www.travelang.com/languages – an online phrasebook with over
60 languages.
www.xe.net.ucc helps you convert all your currency.
www.towd.com the tourism office's worldwide directory.
www.tips4trips.com has travellers' top tips.
www.abtanet.com is the home page for ABTA, the travel industry's
regulatory body.
www.AITO.co.uk is the Association of Independent Tour Operators.

Sites for female travellers

www.journeywoman.com is an online community for travelling women,
including hot tips and newsletters.
www.christinecolumbus.com sells travel products for women, as well as
providing information for travellers.
www.hermail.net is an international network of women travellers
promoting personal connections between women.
www.vagabunda.com has real life travelling tales from women all over
the world.
www.icircle.com/travel has everything from tips for travelling with kids to
flight bargains.
www.handbag.com/travel is the travel channel of the
Handbag.com portal.

Internet-only travel agents

www.expedia.co.uk is Microsoft's huge international travel portal where you can do anything from researching your destination to booking tickets.

www.a2btravel.com

www.bargainholidays.co.uk

www.travelcareonline.com

www.biztravel.com – for the frequent business traveller.

www.deckchair.com

www.lateescapes.com is an auction site for holidays.

www.eurostar.com to book your ticket to the continent.

www.travelocity.co.uk is one of the biggest travel agents on the net.

www.lastminute.com has good last minute deals on flights and holidays.

www.firstresort.com

www.otc-uk.com the Online Travel Company offers some tempting deals, especially late bargains, for destinations across the world.

www.wwj.uk.com or **www.bvi-club.com** specialists in Caribbean dream holidays.

www.laterooms.co.uk – get a cheap hotel room in the UK, at the last minute.

High street travel agents online

www.thomson.co.uk

www.thomascook.com

www.airtours.com

www.first-choice.com

www.going-places.co.uk

www.kuoni.co.uk

www.statravel.co.uk specialises in youth and independent travel.

www.trailfinders.co.uk is a well-known independent travel agency.

Budget airlines and flight-only deals

www.buzzaway.com
www.go-fly.com
www.easyjet.com
www.ryanair.com
www.britishairways.com
www.priceline.com lets you name your own price for flights and hotel rooms: you wait for travel agents to take you up on it!
www.cheapflights.com will find you a flight bargain.
www.ebookers.com is the first place to look for discounted flights. They specialise in discount booking offers – worth a visit by bargain hunters.

Online guidebooks and travel books

www.concierge.com is the website for the glossy Conde Nast traveller magazine.
www.fodors.com is the website for the Fodor's range of guidebooks.
www.goodholidayguide.com
www.which.net/holiday is Which's online guide to holidays.
www.lonelyplanet.com is the homepage of the Lonely Planet guidebooks, and will give you the real low-down on your destination.
www.nationalgeographic.com
www.roughguides.com, a comprehensive site for backpackers and independent travellers.
www.opinionatedtraveller.com read other travellers' forthright views on destinations.
www.salon.com/travel has interesting international travel writing from Salon Magazine.
www.travelchannel.com is a huge online travel resource from the Travel Channel.
www.frommers.com is the famous guides' online presence.
www.timeout.com has the best city guides on the market, now online.
www.africaonline.com has all the travel information you need if you're thinking of going to Africa.
www.planetrider.com is a directory of all the net's travel resources.

Maps

www.mapsworldwide.co.uk
www.multimap.com
www.mapquest.com

Finding a cybercafe

www.cybercafe.com
www.cybercaptive.com
www.cybercafes.com
www.cyberiacafe.net
www.netcafeguide.com

Or if you're away in the UK, check out the unique directory at the back of this book!

Skiing links

www.skiclub.co.uk is the homepage of the Ski Club of Great Britain.
www.skinet.com/ski is Ski Magazine online.
www.1ski.com
www.ski-deals.co.uk
www.skicentral.com is the ultimate skiing portal, with listings of all the sites you need to find the resort you what.
www.skichalets.co.uk

Adventure holidays

www.abercrombiekent.co.uk
www.adventure-mag.com
www.escaperoutes.com
www.i-to-i.com offers voluntary work abroad if you need to stretch your legs.
www.safarilink.com with links to 12 African tourist offices plus advice on health and clothing.

Chapter 24

Celebrations

Everyone loves a party and the chance to celebrate. So what could be better than using the internet to organise everything, giving you time to relax and get ready? From christenings to weddings, all you need to do is log on, and you can find a venue, order and despatch a gift, however rare or unusual, even send greeting cards. And when it comes to getting people together, forget the hassle of phoning round, you can use the net to send your invitations and track your RSVPs. You can even post the photographs on the net afterwards, for your guests to enjoy – or wince.

Virtual cards

If you've just remembered someone's birthday, heard some great news or just want to say hello, one of the most fun uses of the internet is the virtual greetings card, from sites like **www.bluemountain.com**. There are cards for all occasions, from weddings to Christmas, free of charge, at the click of a mouse, and you can personalise your message. Even better, you can send a bunch of virtual flowers from **www.eflowers.com**.

No wonder sending virtual greetings is one of the most popular activities for women online, according to a survey by MMXI Europe.

www.sharpcards.com offer a great service; you can buy real cards from their huge selection, as well as gift vouchers. They will deliver the card to you, or on your behalf. They'll even e-mail you to remind you of important dates!

Hot Tips – Sending e-greetings

1 Go to the website and choose your greeting, such as a birthday or romance from the selection

2 View the cards by clicking on the category you are interested in. Most sites display a range of the cards available for you to download

3 Choose a card and then enter the e-mail address of the person you want to send the card to

4 Add your own personal message and greetings into the card

5 Preview and edit your card. If you are not happy with the way it looks you can change it. When you are ready click on the 'Send' button

6 It is useful to request notification when the recipient views the card, for peace of mind. Keeping a copy of the card is also handy in case you want to send it again

   It's really that easy!

Case Study
Ronnie Sandham

"For the last 25 years, I have been the organiser of the Malcolm Wilson car rally, a very popular annual event for rallying fans and competitors. For the past 2 or 3 years, there has also been a website and e-mail address for the rally, at **www.malcolmwilson.co.uk**, which we have found very useful as an information source for people interested in the event. The site is quite large, and features maps, spectator information and news updates. It's a handy resource for rally fans, because they can find out everything they need to know about the event easily, and can even e-mail me if they need to.

"Year 2000 saw the first use of a web-based tracking system in one of the course cars, one which has now been adopted commercially. This year will see the first mobile text message update of results to competitors, and anyone interested, throughout the event.

"We post event results after the end of the rally even putting photos, video clips and sound bites of the cars on the site! Having a website for an event like this means the rally will reach a wider audience than perhaps it would have done without being on the internet. It's a really easy way to have all the information in one place. We've found that since we started the site, usage has been steadily increasing each year, as more rally fans get online and view our site."

Gifts galore

Tracking down the perfect gift can be time consuming and stressful especially at Christmas. But bringing a smile to the face of even the fussiest friend or relative has never been easier. Instead of trekking down the high street in search of the perfect gift, do your shopping on the net. You can give almost anything, from anywhere in the world, and it's so much less effort. It does pay to be organised so that you have plenty of time to get the gift delivered. You can even get it gift-wrapped and sent straight to the recipient. How's that for convenience?

For spontaneous surprises that everyone will love, head for one of the many gift sites like **www.codygifts.com**, where you'll find all sorts of bargains, from cosmetics and perfumes to flowers. You'll even find sports gear and gadgets for the men in your life. For more on gifts, check out the listings at the end of this chapter, or see the *Shopping Guide* chapter.

Web Life – Organising a good time, online

* Keep all your friends up to date with the party plans on a party home page at **www.evite.com**
* Keep in touch using e-mailed cards – more special than plain e-mail. Try **www.bluemountain.com**
* Order party supplies online – help it go with a bang! **www.iparty.com**
* Keep your wedding list online at **www.debenhams.co.uk**
* Find the right suppliers, at the best prices, through the net. Try **www.shopsmart.com**

Party pieces

The interactivity of the internet is perfect to use when throwing a party. The online party planning sites like **www.evite.com** let do as much or as little as you want. You can send out virtual invitations to your friends by e-mail, and let the site collect the RSVPs for you. Guests can log on to the event's homepage to find out more details, such as directions to the venue. You can even collect payments electronically through the site!

It's really fun to set up an online photo album to display party photos that everyone can access. Either use the photo albums on party sites, or try photo sites like **www.fotango.com**, which will even develop your film and distribute copies for you!

Whatever type of celebration you are planning, the wide selection of food and drink sites are sure to satisfy, from supermarkets, to recipe sites, to online off-licences, to speciality retailers. Best of all, everything you need can be delivered direct to your home.

Make sure your party sparkles by stocking up on some mouth-watering foods, a few bottles of champagne and the best wines at **www.chateauonline.com** or **www.virginwines.com**. On the net you'll find a great choice, special treats at smaller online stores and some excellent bargains, especially if you buy by the case. Forget the heavy shopping – take a seat and let it all come to you.

Wedding bliss

As anybody who has ever done it will tell you, it's hard work getting married. So don't get stressed, get online and let the net take some of the strain. You can do everything, from browsing through dress designs and looking for local venues to finding a special deal on disposable cameras. There are several wedding websites, for example **www.weddingsonline.co.uk**, which not only offers expert advice and a great list of specialist services but can give you inspiration for such tricky matters as speeches, etiquette and honeymoon destinations. You can even keep your wedding list online. Many of the larger department stores like **www.debenhams.co.uk** offer an online service, which your guests can access at their convenience. The gifts will be despatched to you in exactly the same way as if they had been bought from the store itself, and you can log on to your list from the internet.

You know it's time to log on when:

- You want to order some wine without all the hassle of carrying it
- You've got six weeks until the wedding and you haven't finalised anything
- You've forgotten a birthday and need to get a card sorted out, fast
- You've run out of party ideas

Case Study
Amanda Perry

"I got married in September 2000 – it was great! Everything went to plan, everyone looked perfect, and I am now happily married. It's so hard to believe it all went so smoothly, when you consider the time and effort that this one day took to plan, starting on the day of our engagement when a hundred and one questions started racing through my mind – what am I going to wear? What's the groom going to wear? Not to mention the bridesmaids, best man and ushers! Where can we have the reception? Who is supposed to pay for what? Before I got too stressed-out, I got onto the internet to see how it could help me out.

"I was not (and am still not!) an expert on the internet, but with a little guidance I set off in search of some help. **www.confetti.com** was the first site I entered, which gave me so many of the answers to all my questions. There were detailed lists of things to do which gave me an excellent starting point. I also used **www.google.com** to help me in my search for reception venues, dress and suit hire shops, Rolls Royce hire, overnight accommodation for our guests – I could even put the website addresses of each hotel on the wedding invitation. Searching like this saved me days of phoning around. Most importantly, e-mail was an excellent way to keep reminding my now husband that he had still not done all his jobs!"

Don't panic!

Organising a celebration, especially Christmas and weddings, can send even the most organised person into a panic, and may mean you don't enjoy the big day itself! Luckily, the internet lets you instantly and cheaply get in touch with five or 500 people, track down the right gifts, stock up on party essentials and help bring the party spirit into everyone's lives. In fact, with so many sites and services, your only challenge now is that you may be spoilt for choice!

Party sites

Greetings cards

www.bluemountain.com the site offers a huge selection cards for every occasion.
http://uk.greetings.yahoo.com – another excellent service from Yahoo!
www.blab.com for fun cards.
www.e-greetings.com and **www.egreetings.com** has virtual cards for every occasion.
www.sharpcards.com to buy cards online.
www.zjtcards.com sells beautiful cards featuring photographs of real places.
www.e-cards.com will donate money to wildlife charities when you send a card.

Party planning

www.theplunge.com is a complete party resource. Just pick the kind of event you're throwing (eg. birthday party) or use the random party generator to find everything you need to throw the perfect party!
www.iparty.com lets you buy party supplies (like printed balloons) and get a fun themed atmosphere.
www.evite.com will take the pain out of party planning. Build an online social calendar with your friends, or buy supplies for your event.
www.partyparties.co.uk – register to find a party to go to, or get help organising one of your own.
http://uk.invites.yahoo.com lets you send personalised invitations, track RSVPs and even send your own photos as e-greetings cards.

Weddings

www.all-about-weddings.co.uk has great information about planning and enjoying your big day.

www.hitched.co.uk is the definitive wedding website, with advice for the bride, groom, bridesmaids and ushers.

www.confetti.com has the answers to every possible wedding dilemma plus useful information on everything from dresses and photography to cakes and hiring services.

www.webwedding.co.uk helps you add witty quotations to your wedding with its section on speech making.

www.debenhams.co.uk has an online wedding list service – access your own list from the net, and your guests can buy online too!

www.theweddinglist.org.uk is the website of the famous London Wedding List Company shop. Once you've registered, guests can browse your list and buy online.

www.coolwhite.com is a wide-ranging guide to achieving the perfect wedding, with a supplier's directory covering everything from bridesmaid's dresses to booking the honeymoon.

www.weddingguide.co.uk has a comprehensive wedding directory and a well-used discussion forum so you can share the stress with other brides-to-be.

www.wedding-pages.co.uk will help you find local wedding suppliers, searching by postcode.

www.cocky-hen.com will send you naughty novelties for your hen night.

Gifts

www.virtualpresents.com, since it's the thought that counts!

www.codygifts.com is the ultimate online gift solution. It has a huge range with something for everyone. An automatic gift advisor will help you if you get stuck!

www.thegadgetshop.com has free delivery on all gifts.

www.hallmark.com

www.mailacake.co.uk to send a rich fruitcake iced with your own personal message.

www.tiffany.com for great jewellery and quality gifts.

www.giftdeliveryco.com – fun and unusual activity-based gifts.

www.giftstore.co.uk

www.giftinspiration.com

www.propagangsta.com has fun, young novelty gifts like inflatable armchairs.

www.hugsandcuddles.co.uk specialising in teddy bears.

www.alt-gifts.co.uk sells alternative gifts in a wide price range.

www.boxedup.co.uk has stylish and unusual gifts.

www.directcosmetics.com for an extensive selection of bargain perfumes.

www.needapresent.co.uk will cover all your gift needs.

www.interflora.co.uk to say it with flowers.

www.kitbag.com is ideal for the man who loves football, cricket or rugby.

www.firebox.com for all kinds of toys for boys.

Food and drink

www.800hampers.com the ideal site for hampers stuffed full of Scottish goodies, like smoked salmon, shortbread, whiskey and haggis.

www.porcini.co.uk a fabulous range of Mediterranean specialities such as cheeses and hams.

www.lobster.co.uk can add a little luxury and indulgence to any party with its luxury party packs – with nuts, pretzels and exquisite Christmas hampers available

www.oddbins.co.uk has an extensive range of wines along with some special treats for champagne lovers. And if you buy more 12 bottles you can benefit from some great delivery deals.

www.madaboutwine.com has over 4,000 wines at prices to suit everyone.

www.sundaytimeswineclub.com works hard to find the best bargains from around the world for its members.

www.chateauonline.co.uk is the UK's wine specialist on the internet.

www.harrods.com

www.selfridges.com

Chapter 25

Having Fun on the Internet

There are plenty of laughs and fun to be had on the internet that go far beyond your friends e-mailing you the latest jokes. From catching up with the latest celebrity gossip to finding out your day's horoscopes and reading your favourite magazines online, there are so many bright and funky pages that bring fun to you anytime you like!

It's amazing what you'll be able to find even if you're just browsing. Setting off on the internet with no particular destination in mind can be very educational! Try starting in one of the search directories, like Yahoo!, and click on links which take your fancy – you'll be amazed what you turn up! Surfing like this can be incredibly addictive – hours will have passed and you'll still be glued to your screen. It's a lot less passive than slumping in front of the TV though, and you're bound to learn something interesting!

Horoscopes

A secret indulgence all women seem to enjoy, horoscopes are now online. There are an uncountable number of horoscope and prediction sites online, so log on to find out how your day's going to go, or if you need help making a decision you're ambivalent about. It's just a bit of fun, but as we all know, sometimes horoscopes are spookily accurate. Log onto Excite's horoscope directory at **www.excite.co.uk/horoscopes** for links to all kinds of horoscope sites. You can even find out your relationship compatibility. Similarly, **http://astrology.yahoo.com** has a dream analysis page, where you can enter keywords to understand your dreams and find out what your subconscious is trying to tell you. There are also fun tools like palm reading, tarot cards and even an e-crystal ball.

Gaming and gambling on the net

Computer gaming and gambling have become much more appealing to women, thanks to the internet. No more intimidating, smoky bookies shops, now you can place a bet, tax free, from your PC. **www.willhill.com** offers all the usual sports betting online, plus more fun bets like 'who shot Phil Mitchell? **www.flutter.com** lets you place one-to-one bets against other individuals for small amounts – just for fun – on anything from sport to the Oscars!

Computer games are also being enhanced by the internet – players can now compete with each other online, on multiplayer games like Doom and Quake. There are also loads of simpler games on offer for free, like solitaire, Scrabble and chess. The added interactivity of the internet means that playing computer games is more sociable and fun. Try sites like **www.freearcade.com** and **www.gamesville.com** to get started.

Case Study
Sarah Lynch

"I've been using the internet for a couple of years now, since I started using it at work and now I'm also a keen surfer in my lunchbreak. I mostly use it for e-mail, to keep in touch with friends and to get fun things sent to me. I have two separate accounts – I use Yahoo! Mail at **http://mail.yahoo.co.uk** for all my personal e-mails, and hotmail at **www.hotmail.com** to join mailing lists. Having different accounts stops my personal inbox from getting clogged up with too much junk mail. I get jokes sent to me every day from **www.passiton.com**, which brightens up my morning a bit! **www.filmunlimited.co.uk** sends me The Guardian's weekly film update, with reviews and information about the latest releases in the cinemas and on video. I can also keep an eye out for holiday bargains, **www.thomascook.co.uk** send me an e-mail with all the latest deals. It's great getting stuff sent to me, so I don't have to track it all down myself!

"For other fun stuff, it's great to get new ringtone and pictures for my mobile phone, from **www.yourmobile.com** and **www.boltblue.com**. There's a huge range of tones available, from golden oldies to the latest chart releases. At the moment, my mobile's playing Winnie the Pooh! I love going on to **www.thespark.com** to do their quizzes. They have a 'death test' which calculates how much longer you've got to live, down to the nearest minute!"

Comedy

The net has become a thriving setting for all kinds of comedy – you're sure to find something which will make you giggle. A famous funny site is at **www.theonion.com**, an American online newspaper running hilariously satirical stories on all kinds of subjects. **www.funny.co.uk** is a huge British comedy portal, with links to other comedy sites on the net.

Magazines and e-zines

The net is a great place to read all your favourite magazines for free!
Sites like **www.vogue.co.uk** have all the content of the magazine, as
well as useful information like fashion directories and archives of past
issues. **www.cosmopolitan.co.uk** is another good magazine site. There
are also a great number of magazines which only exist on the net, called
e-zines. These are well worth looking up, since they get updated more
frequently than magazines, and can be much more specialised. Some of
the most famous American e-zines are **www.salon.com**,
www.slate.com and **www.suck.com**. You can also find a directory of
e-zines at **www.infojump.com**. **www.chickclick.com** is a portal to
some great feisty women's e-zines, like **www.hipmama.com**. The
freedom of speech of the internet means you can often find out things
which wouldn't be able to be printed (for fear of legal action!). You can
get the inside scoop on what's going on in Hollywood at
www.aintitcoolnews.com, where even movie industry heavyweights log
on to keep ahead of the game. **www.drudgereport.com** is a US site run
by journalist Matt Drudge. It was the first place to break the Monica
Lewinsky affair, and many other news stories first surface on this site –
it gets over two million hits a day!

Celebrity gossip

Everyone loves indulging themselves
by finding out what their favourite stars
have been up to. The internet is the
perfect place to get an instant update,
and the number of celebrity focused sites
out there is huge! **www.anorak.co.uk**
prides itself on keeping tabs on the tabloids,
with a daily compendium of all the top news
stories in the UK papers. Prove your dedication
to all things gossip by subscribing to the **www.popbitch.com** celebrity
newsletter, sent straight to your inbox every Wednesday.

The ultimate UK celebrity site has over 1,000 pages, updated 20 times a day, at **www.peoplenews.com**. Now there's no excuse for not knowing who's just split up with whom, or who's going out with whom this week! There's even a directory of celebrity sites, at **www.celebhoo.com**.

All your favourite TV shows and soaps are also on the internet, with official sites and fan sites telling you all the latest news and keeping you up to date with your characters. **www.beeb.co.uk** has links to all your favourite BBC programmes. **www.coronationstreet.co.uk** will help you catch up with the latest goings-on on Corrie.

Web Life – Having fun on the internet

- Look up your own name at a search site like **www.google.com** – you could well already be on the internet without knowing it. Find out how many other people share your name!
- Pick up beautiful screensavers and desktop wallpaper for your computer for free, at **www.webshots.com** – they have hundreds of thousands of beautiful photos to download
- Look up today's weather and long-term forecasts from the Met. Office, at **www.meto.gov.uk**
- Find out which famous people share your birthday, at **www.famousbirthdays.com**
- Read more about Mahir, the net's first celebrity, who became famous for his unintentionally funny website and is now recording an album. Get the full story from **www.ikissyou.org**

Silly sites

An eye-opening insight into the internet boom is the huge number of really useless or silly sites there are on the net – these sites are great fun, but generally serve no purpose other than to amuse you. There's a great directory of useless sites, at **www.worstoftheweb.com**. Or log on to the famous Centre for the Easily Amused, at **www.amused.com**, which is the ultimate resource for wasting time online. You can create a cyber pet to play with, or read funny stories of other people's horror jobs, plus hundreds of other things to waste your time on! **www.80s.com** is a fun site if you're feeling nostalgic for the 80s, with everything from music quizzes to classic games like Pac Man!

Quizzes and tests.

Similarly, the interactivity of the internet means that quiz sites are incredibly popular. You can do all kinds of quizzes online, from trivia to serious personality tests – do the tests online and get the results right away. Try **www.quizbox.com** for the best in personality tests, or do fun tests like 'the love test' on **www.thespark.com**. There's even a quiz directory called 'test junkie', at **www.queendom.com/test_col.html**. One of the biggest test sites, **www.allthetests.com**, has everything from measuring your emotional intelligence, to testing your chocolate knowledge! If you're brainy, **www.mindbreakers.com** has mind-bending quizzes to test your powers of lateral thought.

Case Study
Lucie Denyer

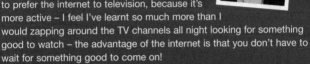

"I first started using the internet at work to do research and find out things, but once I got the hang of it, I realised what fun the net could be for leisure time as well! Now I spend as much time surfing at the weekends and in the evenings as I spend watching TV. I'm starting to prefer the internet to television, because it's more active – I feel I've learnt so much more than I would zapping around the TV channels all night looking for something good to watch – the advantage of the internet is that you don't have to wait for something good to come on!

"My favourite sites are **www.yahoo.com** and **www.yahoo.co.uk** – which has a 'cool links' section that gets updated regularly. This is the best place to look up the huge collection of random and bizarre sites out there, some of them are hilarious! I like to play games at **www.freearcade.com** because it helps me relax. **www.radio1.com** keeps me up to date with the latest music news and reviews.

"I find browsing the internet can be very addictive! Sometimes I just go online without a particular plan and see what I can find – three hours later I'm still engrossed. It's worth the higher phone bills though – the internet is so big, there's something for everyone to keep them entertained, no matter what they're interested in. I like travelling, so sometimes I look up different destinations and start making plans for my next holiday. It's great to have access to so much information, because it's so stimulating, and I often have great ideas which are sparked off by something I've seen on the internet."

You know it's time to log on when:

- You want to be entertained and there's nothing on TV
- The Grand National's coming up and you have a hot tip
- You've missed EastEnders all week and need to find out the latest on Phil Mitchell
- You want to find out what your stars hold in store for you

Fun sites

Quizzes on the net

www.queendom.com/test_col.html is a huge directory of all the quizzes available on the net, filtered into categories. You'll be amazed what you can test for!

www.allthetests.com has a test for everything, from measuring your emotional intelligence to testing your expertise on chocolate bars!

www.mindbreakers.com has mind-bending quizzes to boost your powers of lateral thought.

www.thespark.com has funny tests – their famous Personality Test has been taken by over three million people!

www.quizbox.com has a large collection of quizzes on everything from sports trivia to love tests.

Gossip sites

www.peoplenews.com has the most up-to-date UK celebrity gossip, with over 1,000 pages updated 20 times a day.

www.eonline.com has daily film, TV, and music updates from the US.

www.showbizwire.com has coverage of everything to do with showbusiness, updated constantly.

www.aintitcoolnews.com has the inside scoop on everything that's happening in Hollywood. Log on, and be the first to find out! Similar Hollywood sites include **www.variety.com** and **www.cinescape.com**. **www.anorak.co.uk** is a useful round-up of all the UK papers, including all the tabloids. Indulge your guilty gossip addiction in secret!

Online magazines and e-zines

www.company.co.uk
www.cosmopolitan.co.uk
www.goodhousekeeping.co.uk
www.harpersandqueen.co.uk
www.swoon.co.uk
www.she.co.uk
www.hello-magazine.co.uk
www.marieclaire.com
www.tatler.co.uk
www.vogue.co.uk
www.womensown.co.uk

www.hipmama.com is an e-zine for mothers with attitude!
www.slate.com is MSN's own e-zine, focusing on politics.
www.salon.com is a wide-ranging and intelligent e-zine including a great section called 'mothers who think', and stimulating articles on the arts and politics.
www.suck.com is a funny and satirical e-zine with daily updates on random subjects.
www.theonion.com is probably the funniest and most famous e-zine, with hilarious and bizarre articles on anything and everything.
www.drudgereport.com
www.chickclick.com is a collection of e-zines for feisty women.
www.newsrack.com is a UK directory of all online publications around the world.

www.confused.co.uk is the online presence of Dazed and Confused magazine.

www.bust.com is a humour site with a feminist angle, with forthright and funny articles, links and chatrooms for women.

www.infojump.com has an article search engine which goes through over five million articles from 4,000 publications!

TV shows

www.beeb.co.uk is the BBC's portal to all its shows.

www.livingtv.com has the homepage for the Jerry Springer show.

www.yahoo.co.uk will send you personalised local TV listings, or try **www.unmissabletv.com** or **www.radiotimes.beeb.com** – you'll never miss your favourite show again!

www.bbc.co.uk/eastenders – get an Albert Square update from your computer.

www.coronationstreet.co.uk and **www.corrie.net** are the two best Coronation Street sites.

www.emmerdale.co.uk is the official Emmerdale site; **www.emmerdale.clara.net** is the fan site.

www.brookie.co.uk keep up to date with Brookside Close – even buy Brookie merchandise!

www.hollyoaks.com

Horoscopes and astrology sites

www.horoscope.com has daily updates for your star sign, from the ivillage portal.

www.astrology.com will e-mail you your daily predictions.

www.future365.com is a UK horoscope site.

www.russelgrant.com is the homepage of everyone's favourite astrologer, Russell Grant.

www.astrology-online.com

www.excite.co.uk/horoscopes is Excite's horoscopes directory.

http://astrology.yahoo.com is Yahoo's astrology channel.

Comedy sites

www.joke.co.uk have a joke of the day they will e-mail you.
www.funny.co.uk
www.theonion.com is a hilarious satirical newspaper.
www.passiton.com
www.comedyzone.beeb.co.uk is the BBC's comedy site.
www.hahabonk.com has amusing mini-films.
www.frenchandsaunders.com is a French and Saunders fan site.
www.comicrelief.org.uk is the homepage of Comic Relief.

Gambling online

www.willhill.com is the online betting site from William
Hill, tax-free.
www.bananalotto.com lets you enter a free daily lottery.
www.flutter.com lets you place fun bets against other
individuals.
www.bet247.co.uk
www.bet.co.uk is Ladbrokes online gambling site.
www.thedailydraw.com is a free lottery site, giving away £1 million
a day.
www.national-lottery.co.uk is the official page of the National Lottery.

The Future Online

The net is set to become an even more important part of our lives; today is just the beginning of a great online adventure. Women young and old are joining the internet club faster than any other demographic group. This interactive communications tool will continue to change millions of lives. More women are set to join this revolution that steps far beyond the internet and helps us become empowered.

New careers have already been opened up; and industries and jobs that have historically been male dominated, like technology, are now attracting more women. The skills shortage in technology, coupled with new flexible working practices are making it easier for women to progress in their careers, with successful role models like Martha Lane Fox from **www.lastminute.com** filling our media and dismissing old-fashioned stereotypes of working women. The challenge is to use the potential of internet development to work towards actively removing glass ceilings at the office, and create a better work/life balance for women. The potential is here for us to shape the future and benefit from the internet's ability to accelerate positive change in our personal and professional lives.

An example of the benefits the empowered internet brings women would be the proliferation of women's networking forums as a focal point for us to come together to lobby for change. More and more women are discovering the advantages of getting together on- and offline to help each other, to support career development, build confidence and opportunities. This is the time for women to use the internet for a new style of positive feminism, where people from diverse backgrounds come together and share the same opportunities.

What happens next?

Sheila Sang, Editorial Director of **www.handbag.com**, believes our screens will never be the same again: "By 2005 it's predicted that the majority of the western European population will be online, and that half of us will be using more than one device – be it PC, phone, TV or Personal Digital Assistant to get online. Shopping and research will continue to bring and keep us online, particularly for women juggling work and family. Supermarket shopping – still clunky at the moment – is bound to take off. From books to CDs, clothes, shoes and breakfast cereal, many of us will move to making the majority of our purchases online. High-speed broadband connection will make all this easier. Not only will you be able to view sites quickly, you'll also get good quality audio and video on your PC."

These new devices will bring the net even closer to our lives. Online access on the move will become so commonplace even a computer shy person will find themselves with easy ways to access thousands of sites.

Internet services will also become commonplace through TV sets, making our viewing interactive and transactional. Your TV set will no longer sit in the corner of the room just showing your favourite programmes – it's already going digital. Over five million households in the UK have already made the switch from analogue. And more families are set to go interactive. By connecting a set-top box and phone line you will be able to send e-mails, check your bank balance and even order pizza with your remote control!

The mobile internet will grow, too. Over the next twelve months or so a new generation of phones and technology will allow fast access to information, with location-based services checking all kinds of useful information on your phone or Personal Digital Assistant. Mobile phones will deliver m-commerce and interactive TV. Gartner group even predicts that by 2010, 75% of teenagers will have wearable computing and communications devices!

And, importantly, we'll probably get used to turning to friends in bulletin boards and chatrooms for advice on a huge range of topics, getting the information either online or through the phone or PDA.

This is just the start, the mobile internet is developing every day. The future is online and the good news is that the net is already empowering lots of women. UK Web Women are finding internet inspiration in all parts of their lives. Let's enjoy this great adventure!

Web predictions

- Internet technology and access will continue to improve, with bandwidth and costs becoming even more attractive

- The number of women online is set to surpass men worldwide as it already has done in the US

- More jobs, more opportunities for women online are set to have a positive impact on our lives

- Mobile internet and second-generation web devices will open up the internet to millions of new surfers

- The internet will be a mainstream part of every business, with more companies realising the benefits of linking to suppliers and customers online

- The real winners online will be the companies with strong business plans that can make a profit

- Bricks and mortar companies are set to win even more battles online and become the dominant online brands

- The dot com fever will not return, replaced by realistic outlooks based on brand values, realistic business models and strong management

- The shortage in skilled workers in the technology sector will create more diverse job opportunities

- There will be more opportunities for 'e-lancers' in the job market, with more companies employing contractors with flexible work packages

- Home working is on the rise and set to make a significant increase in coming years

The future generation

In the future our challenge is to ensure that everyone has the opportunity to experience the net, and that girls and boys from all backgrounds have access to its opportunities as early as possible. Similarly, older generations from every walk of life can broaden their horizons online. The future is about providing education and training, and ensuring we give everyone equal opportunity to benefit from the internet.

Promoting 'internet for schools' initiatives and capturing the enthusiasm of kids at a young age is essential. Computing and internet studies should be built into the curriculum of every school with internet access and facilities being backed by major corporate and government investment. The Government has already made a commitment to get every school connected to the internet by the end of 2002.

The future is about helping everyone to reap the benefits of being connected. We have to ensure that our children actively embrace computers and technology, creating more diverse opportunities for everyone.

The internet is here to stay and offers endless opportunities in all parts of our lives. It is still early days, so be inquisitive and explore the net to discover the possibilities.

Why not share you experiences with other women on www.ukwebwomen.com?

Use the net to liberate yourself, and enjoy it along the way.

101 Things to do on the net

Happy surfing

Free internet advice	www.myhelpdesk.com
Upgrade your PC	www.jungle.com
E-mail on the move	www.hotmail.com
Search and find	www.google.com
Put safety first	www.netnanny.com
Stop junk mail	www.junkbusters.com
Ask a good question	www.ask.co.uk
Avoid a virus	www.vmyths.com

Go shopping

High street brands at home	www.zoom.co.uk
Get a bargain	www.unbeatable.co.uk
Order a new outfit	www.indigosquare.co.uk
Update your music collection	www.cdnow.com
Get the best price	www.checkaprice.co.uk
Buy a car	www.jamjar.com
Name your own price	www.ebay.co.uk

Spoil yourself

Mix the perfect cocktail	www.mixology.com
Fill the fridge	www.tesco.com
Cook like a chef	www.jamieoliver.net
Stock up on wine	www.oddbins.co.uk
Have an organic experience	www.organicsdirect.com
Chocolates for you	www.thorntons.co.uk

Home service

Do it yourself	www.homebase.co.uk
Transform your garden	www.bbc.co.uk/gardening
Keep the kids happy	www.kidsevents.co.uk
Help with the homework	www.ajkids.com
Enjoy parenthood	www.motherandbaby.co.uk
Find the perfect plumber	www.referenceline.co.uk
Get the number	www.phonenumbers.net

Get moving

Move house	www.pickfords.co.uk
Drive a bargain motor	www.autotrader.co.uk
Plan your route	www.theaa.co.uk
Find a house	www.propertyfinder.co.uk

Be healthy

Give up smoking	www.ash.com
Join a gym	www.health-club.net
Kick the habit	www.trashed.co.uk
Talk to a doctor	www.drkoop.com
Be flexible	www.yogasite.com
Eat well	www.mynutrition.com

Be generous

Be charitable	www.free2give.co.uk
Give the perfect gift	www.tiffany.com
Place a bid	www.qxl.co.uk
Throw a party	www.theplunge.com
Send a virtual gift	www.virtualpresents.com

Travel easy

Price your own holiday	www.priceline.com
Visit a exotic destination	www.tropical.co.uk
Enjoy the snow	www.skicentral.com
Get the lowdown on your destination	www.lonelyplanet.com
Book a bargain flight	www.buzzaway.com
Get a last minute deal	www.lastminute.com

Money matters

Make your money work harder	www.if.co.uk
Save on mortgage payments	www.hotmortgage.co.uk
Handy tax advice	www.inlandrevenue.gov.uk
Become a stockbroker	www.etrade.co.uk
Money for ideas	www.ideadollar.com
Pay as you go	www.splashplastic.com

Activate your brain cells

Upgrade your skills	www.learndirect.co.uk
Take a distance learning course	www.open.ac.uk
Learn the lingo	www.linguaphone.co.uk
Get an online lawyer	www.desktoplawyer.net
Learn a new skill	www.ehow.com
Virtual library	www.libraryspot.com

Get organised
Make a will	www.wills-by-web.co.uk
Subscribe to a mailing list	www.liszt.com
Everything in one place	www.handbag.com
Balance your life	www.flametree.co.uk
Join a networking group	www.busygirl.co.uk
Know your local area	www.upmystreet.com
Keep track of everyone	www.efridge.com

At work
Know your rights	www.womens-unit.gov.uk
Find forward-thinking employers	www.greatplacetowork.co.uk
Keep ahead in business	www.ft.com
Get a new boss	www.monster.com
Try homeworking	www.homeworking.com
Link to the business services you need	www.businesspages.com
Give yourself a career assessment	www.topjobs.co.uk

Chill out
Read a classic novel	www.amazon.co.uk
Feel the groove	www.napster.com
Be an art lover	www.eyestorm.com
Own a cyberpet	www.aibo.com
Relieve the stress	www.howtomanagestress.co.uk
Enjoy the views of London	www.webviews.co.uk
Step back in time	www.thebritishmuseum.ac.uk
Chat about anything	http://chat.yahoo.com
Indulge in celebrity gossip	www.anorak.co.uk
Boost your brain power	www.mindbreakers.com
Get your horoscope e-mailed to you	www.horoscope.com
See a movie	www.imdb.com

Relationships
Send a card	www.bluemountain.com
Trace your ancestors	www.cyndislist.com
Join a club	www.egroups.com
Discuss your opinions	www.deja.com
Find a long-lost friend	www.whowhere.com
Love on the net	www.dating.co.uk
Get a divorce	www.divorce-online.co.uk
Find true love	www.swoon.com

Family fun
Meet the mums	www.mumsnet.com
Get homework help	www.topmarks.co.uk
Enhance your creativity	www.mamamedia.com
Curious kids	www.discovery.com
Pets fun	www.pets-pyjamas.co.uk

www.ukwebwomen.com

Glossary

ADSL (Asymmetric Digital Subscriber Line) a type of digital phone line providing faster internet access.

Attachment: a computer file (for example, a Word document) included in an e-mail and sent electronically.

Backbone: the high-speed network connection between large internet sites.

Bandwidth: Network speed, normally measured in BPS (bits per second), KBPS (kilobits per second) or MBPS (megabits per second).

Banner Ad: an advert placed on a Web page, normally at the top.

Bit: the smallest unit of measure for computer and digital data.

Bookmark: a way to save your favourite webpage addresses on your internet browser so you don't have to remember them.

Bounce: if you use the wrong e-mail address when you write to someone, your e-mail will 'bounce' back to your inbox with an error message.

BPS (Bits per second): a measure of how fast data can be transmitted.

Broadband: high-speed connection to the internet.

Browser: a piece of software used to navigate the World Wide Web.

Byte: eight bits. Used to measure computer memory and disk space

Cache: a record of all the web sites you have visited, stored on your browser.

Chat: to interact with other internet users in virtual meeting-places, called chatrooms.

Cookie: a text file stored on your computer by a web site, which records information about you.

Domain Name: an internet address without the www.

Download: to copy a file from the internet to your computer.

E-mail: electronic messages sent through the internet.

Emoticon: used to portray emotions in typed text: :-).

Extranet: a web site specifically for a company's suppliers and partners.

E-zine: online magazines.

FAQ (Frequently Asked Questions): a document containing the answers to commonly asked questions. Often a section of a Web site.

Flaming: sending rude or angry messages.

Firewall: a system to protect a network connected to the internet from unwanted access eg. hacking.

Home Page: the opening page of a website, used to navigate to other areas of the site.

HTML (Hypertext Markup Language): the main programming language of the World Wide Web.

HyperText Links: a way to connect to another document on the net. Clicking on the link (usually an image or highlighted text) will take you there.

Internet: The world wide interconnection of computers and computer networks.

IRC (Internet Relay Chat): a real-time chat system on the web.

ISP (Internet Service Provider): a company providing services such as access to the internet.

Instant Messaging: instant chat programmes.

Intranet: a company's private internal network, with no public access.

ISDN (Integrated Services Digital Network): a type of digital phone line providing faster internet access.

Java: a programming language invented by Sun Microsystems, which can run on different kinds of computers.

JPEG: a format for images on the net.

Link: a way to connect to another document on the net. Clicking on the link (usually an image or highlighted text) will take you there.

Lurk: to read a mailing list or enter a chat room without participating.

Mailing lists: a type of e-mail newsletter which you can subscribe to.

Modem: the device which connects the phone line to your computer.

MP3: CD-quality music kept in computer files and available from the net.

MPEG: a format for video on the net.

Network: a group of computers which are connected to each other, like the internet itself.

Newsgroup: an internet discussion group. The collection of newsgroups is known as Usenet.

Newsreader: a programme which connects you to Usenet newsgroups.

Page: a document on the World Wide Web containing many different kinds of content.

Platform: Computer operating system, such a Microsoft Windows or Linux.

Portal: a web site used as a starting point when browsing.

PICS (Platform for Internet Content Selection): a rating system for web pages, normally used to make the web safe for kids.

QuickTime: a multimedia file format.

RealAudio: an audio file format, available from **www.real.com**.

Search engine: a programme used to find information on the web.

Secure Server: a web server using encryption to protect sensitive information, such as credit card details.

Server: a computer providing a service to other computers connected to the net. Sun Microsystems' servers power most of the internet.

Shockwave: a format for multimedia on the net. To download the programme, go to **www.shockwave.com**.

Smiley: used to portray emotions in typed text: :-).

Spam: junk e-mail.

Surfing: browsing the net.

Thread: a posting on a mailing list or newsgroup, connected to all related discussions.

Upload: copying information from your computer to the internet.

URL (Uniform Resource Locator): the address of any item available through your browser i.e. a web address.

Usenet: the group of thousands of internet discussion groups.

WAP (Wireless Application Protocol): a device to make the internet accessible from mobile devices like phones.

Webcam: a video camera with footage going directly onto the internet.

Website: a collection of web pages, usually under a common URL.

WWW (World Wide Web): the use of the internet to publish and view hyperlinked documents (i.e. web pages).

www.nationwide.co.uk
www.natwest.co.uk
www.pru.co.uk
www.rbs.co.uk
www.smile.co.uk
www.virgin-direct.co.uk
www.woolwich.co.uk
www.if.co.uk

Books

www.amazon.co.uk.
www.bol.co.uk
www.alphabetstreet.co.uk
www.whsmithonline.co.uk
www.waterstones.co.uk
www.dillons.co.uk
www.stanfords.co.uk
www.audiobooks.co.uk
www.murderone.co.uk
www.zwemmer.co.uk
www.bookshop.co.uk
http://bookshop.blackwells.co.uk
www.books.co.uk
www.bookbrain.co.uk

Business news

www.fastcompany.com
www.ft.com
www.silicon.com

www.redherring.com
www.computerweekly.com
www.cnbc.com
www.cnfn.com
www.economist.com
www.wsj.com

Business services

www.businesspages.com
www.clearlybusiness.com
www.seekingcapital.com
www.business-incubator.com
www.companieshouse.gov.uk

Catalogues

www.boden.co.uk
www.freemans.co.uk
www.grattan.co.uk
www.shoppersuniverse.com
www.hawkshead.com
www.redoute.co.uk
www.landsend.co.uk
www.llbean.com
www.racinggreen.co.uk
www.kaysnet.com
www.argos.co.uk
www.indexshop.com

Celebrity gossip

www.peoplenews.com
www.eonline.com
www.showbizwire.com
www.aintitcoolnews.com
www.variety.com
www.cinescape.com.
www.anorak.co.uk

Chat sites

http://chat.yahoo.com
http://chat.excite.com
http://msn.co.uk
www.thepark.com
www.worlds.net
www.hyperchat.co.uk
www.beefnut.com
www.theglobe.com

Comedy

www.joke.co.uk
www.funny.co.uk
www.theonion.com
www.passiton.com
www.comedyzone.beeb.co.uk
www.hahabonk.com
www.frenchandsaunders.com
www.comicrelief.org.uk

Computers

www.pcpro.co.uk
www.dixons.co.uk
www.comet.co.uk
www.currys.co.uk
www.pcworld.co.uk.
www.unbeatable.co.uk
www.jungle.com

Cooking

www.simplyfood.com
www.bbc.co.uk.foodanddrink
www.therepertoire.com
www.my-meals.com
www.leapingsalmon.com
www.jamieoliver.net
www.nigella.com
www.ichef.com

Cosmetics and health

www.boots.co.uk
www.superdrug.co.uk
www.uk.avon.com
www.thebodyshop.co.uk
www.clinique.com
www.loreal.com
www.olay.com
www.revlon.com
www.tisserand.com

Site Guide Index

www.nivea.co.uk
www.sephora.com
www.yinyang.com
www.bobbibrowncosmetics.com
www.gloss.com
www.crabtree-evelyn.co.uk
www.directcosmetics.com
www.perfumeshopping.com
www.lookfantastic.co.uk
www.iris-online.co.uk
www.drugstore.com
www.allcures.com
www.pharmacy2u.co.uk
www.holistichands.co.uk
www.changeslive.com
www.sweatybetty.co.uk
www.sweatshop.co.uk.

Credit cards

www.americanexpress.co.uk
www.barclaycard.co.uk
www.capitalone.co.uk
www.dinersclub.com
www.egg.com
www.goldfish.com
www.marbles.com
www.cahoot.com
www.mbna.co.uk

Cybercafes

www.cybercafe.com
www.cybercaptive.com
www.cybercafes.com
www.cyberiacafe.net
www.netcafeguide.com

Dating

www.virtuallydating.com
www.match.com
www.love-makers.com
www.one-and-only.com
www.venusdating.co.uk
www.dating.co.uk
www.flirt.com
www.gorgeousgetto
gethers.com
www.bematched.co.uk
www.dateline.co.uk
www.clubsirius.com
www.culturelovers.com
www.onlylunch.co.uk
www.natural-friends.com
www.gliagency.co.uk
www.countrypartners.co.uk
www.friendfinder.com
www.nomorefrogs.com
www.woowho.co.uk
www.totallyjewish.com

Department stores

www.allders.co.uk
www.argos.co.uk
www.bentalls.co.uk
www.bhs.co.uk
www.debenhams.co.uk
www.fortnumandmason.co.uk
www.harrods.com
www.houseoffraser.co.uk
www.indexshop.com
www.johnlewis.co.uk
www.liberty-of-london.com
www.marks-and-spencer.co.uk
www.selfridges.co.uk
www.woolworths.co.uk

Designer bargains

www.designerheaven.co.uk
www.yoox.com
www.intofashion.com
www.theclothestore.com
www.zercon.com
www.zoom.co.uk
www.designerdirect.co.uk
www.haburi.com
www.bluefly.com

Diets and nutrition

www.cyberdiet.com
www.medicinecabinet.co.uk
www.foodwatch.com.au
www.healthcalc.net
www.mynutrition.co.uk
www.weightwatchers.com
www.feelingfat.net

DIY

www.improveline.com.
www.naturalhandyman.com
www.homepro.com
www.referenceline.com.
www.diy.co.uk
www.diyfixit.co.uk
www.diymate.com
www.diy.com

Doctors on the net

www.nhsdirect.nhs.uk
www.drkoop.com.
www.drweil.com
www.drlockie.com
www.netdoctor.co.uk
www.patient.co.uk.
www.e-med.co.uk
www.2psych.com

www.docnet.org.uk
www.onlinesurgery.com
www.24dr.com

E-mail

www.hotmail.com
www.chickmail.com
www.twigger.co.uk
www.nameplanet.com
www.bigfoot.com
www.postmaster.co.uk
www.hushmail.com
www.ziplip.com.
www.emailaddresses.com
www.another.com
www.purpleturtle.com
www.mailround.com
www.zaplet.com
www.eudora.com
www.emoticonuniverse.com
www.anonymizer.com
www.uboot.com

Estate agents

www.winkworths.com
www.foxtons.co.uk
www.underoneroof.com
www.assertahome.com

www.propertyweb.com
www.urbia.com
www.londonhome.net
www.easier.co.uk
www.houseweb.com
www.mooov.com
www.08004homes.com

Film

www.imdb.com
www.popcorn.co.uk
www.filmsunlimited.co.uk
www.radiotimes.com/film

Financial advice

www.iii.com
www.find.co.uk
www.fsa.gov.uk
www.ft.com
www.ftyourmoney.com
www.thisismoney.com
www.fool.co.uk
www.mrscohen.com

Fitness and sport

www.netfit.co.uk
www.atozfitness.com
www.health-club.net

www.bodyisland.com
www.fitnesslink.com
www.active.org.uk
www.yogasite.com
www.runnersworld.com
www.newrunner.com
www.womensrunning.com
www.bodydoctorfitness.com
www.yoga.co.uk
www.yogaplus.co.uk
www.sportsfix.co.uk

Flowers

www.interflora.co.uk
www.flowersbydirect.co.uk
www.giftstore.co.uk
www.giftdelivery.co.uk
www.flowersdirect.co.uk
www.jane-packer.co.uk
www.teleflorist.co.uk

Food and drink

www.800hampers.com
www.lastorders.com
www.porcini.co.uk
www.lobster.co.uk
www.oddbins.co.uk
www.madaboutwine.com

www.sundaytimeswineclub.com
www.chateauonline.co.uk
www.harrods.com
www.selfridges.com

Gambling

www.willhill.com
www.bananalotto.com
www.flutter.com
www.bet247.co.uk
www.bet.co.uk
www.thedailydraw.com
www.national-lottery.co.uk

Gardening

www.bbc.co.uk/gardening
www.gardenersworld.beeb.com
www.rhs.org.uk
www.crocus.co.uk
www.e-garden.co.uk
ww2.garden.com
www.dig-it.co.uk
www.gardenworld.co.uk
www.garden-uks.org.uk
www.yougrowgirl.com

www.zipfax.com
www.gilgordon.com
www.combo.com
www.yac.com
www.tca.org.uk
www.swiftdesk.com

Horoscopes and astrology sites
www.horoscope.com
www.astrology.com
www.future365.com
www.russelgrant.com
www.astrology-online.com.
www.excite.co.uk/horoscopes
http://astrology.yahoo.com

House and home
www.move.co.uk
www.upmystreet.com
www.undermystreet.com
www.homecheck.co.uk
www.pickfords.co.uk
www.smove.com
www.ihavemoved.co.uk
www.goodmigrations.co.uk

Internet Relay Chat
www.mirc.co.uk
www.irchelp.org
www.newircusers.com
www.ircnews.com
http://mirc.stealth.net/mircrulz/

Instant Messaging
www.icq.com
http://free.aol.com/aim
http://messenger.yahoo.com
http://messenger.msn.com

ISPs
www.compuserve.com
www.demon.net
www.easynet.co.uk
www.gemsoft.net
www.genie.co.uk
www.global.net.uk
www.netcom.net.uk
www.netscapeonline.co.uk
www.uk.uu.net
www.breathe.com
www.freeserve.com
www.freeuk.com
www.lineone.net
www.ntl.com
www.screaming.net

www.tesco.net
www.virgin.net
www.x-stream.co.uk
www.handbag.com

Jobs
www.monster.co.uk
www.hotrecruit.co.uk
www.do-it.org.uk
www.workthing.com
www.jobsite.co.uk
www.stepstone.co.uk
www.fish4jobs.co.uk
www.peoplebank.com
www.jobsunlimited.co.uk
www.jobhunter.co.uk
www.i-resign.com
www.agencycentral.co.uk
www.rec.uk.com
www.fledglings.net
www.gradunet.co.uk
www.milkround.co.uk
www.adecco.co.uk
www.reed.co.uk
www.brookstreet.co.uk
www.tempz.com

Kids' sites
www.yahooligans.com
www.surfnetkids.com
www.bbc.co.uk/webguide
www.girltech.com
www.ajkids.com
www.about.com/kids
www.nick.com
www.foxkids.co.uk
www.cartoonnetwork.com.
www.citv.co.uk
www.bbc.co.uk/cbbc
www.warnerbros.com.

Kids' education
www.eduweb.co.uk
www.atschool.co.uk
www.virtualschool.co.uk
www.edview.com
www.funschool.com
www.funbrain.com
www.schoolzone.co.uk
www.learningstore.co.uk
www.dyslexia-information.com
www.projectgcse.co.uk
www.gcse.com
www.revise.it
www.bbc.co.uk/education/
gcsebitesize

Music

www.cdnow.com
www.cd-wow.com
www.clickmusic.co.uk
www.cduniverse.com
www.towereurope.com
www.hmv.co.uk
www.blackstar.co.uk
www.napster.com
www.worldpop.com
www.audiostreet.com
www.nme.com
www.music.com
www.pollstar.com
www.ticketmaster.co.uk
www.ejay.co.uk

Parenting and pregnancy

www.mumsnet.com
www.parents.org.uk
www.practicalparent.org.uk
www.aliaboutparents.com
www.ukmums.co.uk
www.e-mum.com
www.parents-news.co.uk
www.motherandbaby.co.uk
www.childcare-info.co.uk
www.mothercare.com
www.nurserydirect.co.uk

www.babycentre.co.uk
www.chinagold.com
www.babyworld.co.uk
www.motherandbaby.co.uk
www.fitpregnancy.com
www.homebirth.org.uk
www.homebirth.net
www.activebirthcentre.com
www.emmasdiary.co.uk
www.thebabyregistry.co.uk

Party planning

www.theplunge.com
www.iparty.com
www.evite.com
www.partyparties.co.uk
http://uk.invites.yahoo.com

Payment cards

www.uksmart.co.uk
www.rools.com
www.splashplastic.com
www.greenpeasoup.com

Pets

www.thepetcenter.com
www.puppies.co.uk
www.petspark.com
www.petspyjamas.co.uk

www.animalnet.com
www.petemporium.com
www.petsforkids.co.uk

Portals

www.freeserve.com
www.msn.co.uk
www.yahoo.co.uk
www.excite.co.uk
www.zoom.co.uk
www.open.gov.uk
www.about.com
www.imdb.co.uk
www.cnn.co.uk
www.bbc.co.uk
www.schoolzone.co.uk.
www.netdoctor.co.uk
www.moonfruit.com
www.handbag.com
www.ivillage.co.uk
www.ivillage.co.uk
www.beme.com
www.femail.co.uk
www.everywoman.co.uk
www.icircle.com
www.women.com
www.chickclick.com
www.oxygen.com

Quizzes

www.queendom.com
www.allthetests.com
www.mindbreakers.com
www.thespark.com
www.quizbox.com

Romance Sites

www.hullucinations.com
/dearlynda
www.lovestory.com.au
www.swoon.com
www.secretadmirer.com
www.loveisgreat.com
www.inspirationpoint.com
www.1001waystobe
romantic.com
www.cyber-loving.com
www.rom101.com

Safety sites

www.internetwatch.org.uk
www.rsac.org
www.w3.org
www.scambusters.com
www.worldwidescam.com
www.anti-virus.about.com
www.about.com

Site Guide Index

www.wildxangel.com
www.vmyths.com
www.chatdanger.com

Safety – e-commerce
www.oft.gov.uk
www.bizrate.com
www.which.net.
www.ilevel.com
www.isitsafe.com
www.truste.org
www.bbbonline.org
www.verisign.com

Safety – filtering software
www.netnanny.com
www.surfcontrol.com
www.cybersitter.com
www.surfmonkey.com

Safety – privacy
www.dataprotection.gov.uk
www.epic.org
www.mail-abuse.org
www.junkbusters.com

Search directories
www.yahoo.com
www.yahoo.co.uk

www.dmoz.com
www.excite.co.uk
www.looksmart.com
www.looksmart.co.uk
www.northernlight.com
www.ukplus.co.uk
www.ukdirectory.co.uk
www.ukmax.co.uk
www.ukonline.co.uk.
www.yell.com
www.scoot.co.uk
www.about.com

Search Engines
www.alltheweb.com
www.ditto.com
www.altavista.com
www.euroseek.net
www.god.com
www.hotbot.com
www.hotbot.co.uk
www.lycos.com
www.lycos.co.uk
www.infoseek.co.uk
www.raging.com
www.go.com
www.google.com

Search – Metasearchers
www.askjeeves.com
www.askjeeves.co.uk
www.ajkids.com
www.metacrawler.com
www.copernic.com
www.mirago.com
www.mamma.com
www.dogpile.com
www.savvysearch.com
www.alloversearch.com

Search – Other Resources
www.searchenginewatch.com
www.searchengine
showdown.com
www.searchiq.com

Search – people
http://people.scoot.co.uk
www.atchoo.org/search.html
www.whowhere.com
www.peoplesite.com,
www.bigfoot.com,
www.excite.com,
www.altavista.com,
www.four11.com,
www.people.yahoo.com
www.iaf.net.

Search – specialist directories
www.femina.com
www.wwomen.com
www.directoryguide.com
www.searchengineguide.com

Shopping directories
and malls
www.shopgenie.com
www.shopmart.com
www.valuemad.com
www.excite.co.uk/shopping
www.freeserve.com/shopping
www.topoftheshops.co.uk
www.beenz.com
www.checkaprice.com
www.which.net
www.mytaxi.com
www.shopsafe.co.uk
www.shopsmart.com
www.obongo.com
www.ybag.com
www.shoppingunlimited.co.uk
www.priceoffers.co.uk
www.shoppingarcade.co.uk
www.ishop.co.uk
www.dolondon.com

www.indigosquare.com
www.uk.shopping.yahoo.com
www.zoom.co.uk

Silver surfers
www.arp.org.uk
www.ageconcern.co.uk
www.helptheaged.org.uk
www.idf50.co.uk
www.theoldie.co.uk
www.lifebegins.net
www.u3a.org.uk
www.saga.co.uk
www.vienetwork.com
www.vavo.com
www.seniority.co.uk
www.60-plus.co.uk
www.thirdage.com

Skiing
www.goodskiguide.com
www.complete-skier.com
www.skiclub.co.uk
www.skinet.com/ski
www.1ski.com
www.ski-deals.co.uk
www.skicentral.com
www.skichalets.co.uk

Stockbrokers
www.etrade.co.uk
www.barclays-stockbrokers.co.uk
www.xest.com
www.comdirect.co.uk
www.schwab-worldwide.com/europe
www.selftrade.co.uk
www.sharexpress.co.uk
www.nasdaq.com
www.londonstockexchange.com

Supermarkets
www.asda.co.uk
www.budgens.co.uk
www.co-op.co.uk
www.iceland.co.uk
www.morrisons.plc.uk
www.organicsdirect.com
www.purelyorganic.co.uk
www.bbr.co.uk
www.safeway.co.uk
www.sainsburys.co.uk
www.savacentre.co.uk
www.somerfield.co.uk
www.tesco.com
www.waitrose.co.uk

www.thorntons.co.uk
www.leapingsalmon.com
www.lastorders.com
www.chateauonline.co.uk

Tax
www.inlandrevenue.gov.uk
www.tax.org.uk
http://listen.to/taxman

Teen sites
www.girlynation.com
www.razzberry.com
www.bolt.com
www.trouble.co.uk
www.brit-teen.com
www.mykindaplace.com
www.teentalk.org.uk
www.teenfront.com
www.ukteen.com
www.thej.net
www.bbc.co.uk/so
www.adolescentadulthood.com
www.breakupgirl.com
www.thesite.org
www.youth2youth.co.uk
www.lifebyte.com
www.lovelifeuk.com

Teens educational resources
www.gcse.com
www.a-levels.co.uk
www.ucas.ac.uk
www.push.co.uk
www.gapyear.com
www.homeworkhigh.com
www.homeworkelephant.co.uk
www.learn.co.uk

Telephone directories
www.192.com
www.bt.com/phonenetuk
www.yell.com
www.thornweb.co.uk
www.scoot.co.uk
www.phonenumbers.net
www.royalmail.com

Television
www.beeb.co.uk
www.livingtv.com
www.yahoo.co.uk
www.unmissabletv.com
www.radiotimes.beeb.com
www.bbc.co.uk/eastenders
www.coronationstreet.co.uk
www.corrie.net
www.emmerdale.co.uk

Site Guide Index

www.emmerdale.clara.net
www.brookie.co.uk
www.hollyoaks.com

Travel agents

www.expedia.co.uk
www.a2btravel.com
www.bargainholidays.co.uk
www.travelcareonline.com
www.biztravel.com
www.deckchair.com
www.lateescapes.com
www.eurostar.com
www.travelocity.co.uk
www.lastminute.com
www.firstresort.com
www.otc-uk.com
www.wwj.uk.com
www.bvi-club.com
www.laterooms.co.uk
www.thomson.co.uk
www.thomascook.com
www.airtours.com
www.first-choice.com
www.going-places.co.uk
www.kuoni.co.uk
www.statravel.co.uk
www.trailfinders.co.uk

Travel guides

www.concierge.com
www.fodors.com
www.goodholidayguide.com
www.which.net/holiday
www.lonelyplanet.com
www.nationalgeographic.com
www.roughguides.com
www.opinionatedtraveller.com
www.salon.com/travel
www.travelchannel.com
www.frommers.com
www.timeout.com
www.africaonline.com
www.planetrider.com

Travel resources

www.fco.gov.uk/travel
www.travelang.com/languages
www.xe.net.ucc
www.towd.com
www.tips4trips.com
www.abtanet.com
www.AITO.co.uk

University

www.student-world.co.uk
www.nus.org.uk
www.yoonee.com
www.studyoverseas.com
www.helpineedto.co.uk
www.student123.com

Underwear online

www.splendour.com
www.figleaves.com
www.rigbyandpeller.co.uk
www.smartbras.com
www.knickerbox.co.uk
www.bravissimo.com

Usenet

www.deja.com
www.newsguy.com
www.supernews.com
www.newzbot.com
www.faqs.org
www.tile.net

Weddings

www.all-about-weddings.co.uk
www.hitched.co.uk
www.confetti.com
www.webwedding.co.uk
www.debenhams.co.uk
www.theweddinglist.org.uk
www.coolwhite.com
www.weddingguide.co.uk
www.wedding-pages.co.uk
www.cocky-hen.com

Women's health sites

www.womens-health.com
www.icircle.com/health
www.fpa.org.uk.
www.healthsquare.com
www.healthyideas.com
www.women.com
www.ivillage.co.uk/health.
www.handbag.com/health.
www.lovelife.com
www.gyn101.com
www.obgyn.net.

274

Women's networking groups

www.busygirl.co.uk
www.hightech-women.com
www.womens-institute.org.uk
www.advancingwomen.com
www.digital-women.com
www.nwr.org
www.amazoncity.com/chat
www.phoenix-network.org
www.digitaleveuk.org
www.flametree.co.uk
www.e-womenforum.com
www.ukwebwomen.com

Women's portals

www.handbag.com
www.ivillage.com
www.ivillage.co.uk
www.beme.com
www.femail.co.uk
www.everywoman.co.uk
www.icircle.com
www.women.com
www.chickclick.com
www.oxygen.com

Women travellers

www.journeywoman.com
www.christinecolumbus.com
www.icircle.com/travel
www.hermail.net
www.vagabunda.com

Working Women

www.busygirl.co.uk
www.eoc.org.uk
www.dti.gov.uk/er
www.the-bag-lady.co.uk
www.opportunitynow.org.uk
www.womenback2work.co.uk
www.womenreturners.org.uk
www.parentsatwork.org.uk
www.networkingmoms.com
www.childcarelink.gov.uk
http://womenswire.com/work/
www.workingwoman.com
www.womens-unit.gov.uk
www.set4women.gov.uk
www.hse.gov.uk
www.digital-women.com
www.businessadviceonline.org
www.businesslink.co.uk
www.thebiz.co.uk
www.smartbiz.com

www.clearlybusiness.com
www.scottishbusiness
women.com
www.wellpark.com

Work/Life balance

www.lifeminders.com
www.en-parent.com
www.jugglezine.com
www.worklifebalance.co.uk
www.worklifeforum.com
www.new-ways.co.uk
www.efridge.com
www.ivillage.co.uk/workcareer
www.everywoman.co.uk.
www.self-growth.com

Chapter 30

Cybercafes

Even if you are not planning to buy a computer immediately, you'll still be able to use the internet at public access points like cybercafes and libraries.

The number of libraries with internet access is set to grow hugely, due to the Government's commitment to get all 4,300+ public libraries across the UK online by 2002! This is part of the UK Online initiative, which aims to ensure that everyone in the UK who wants to be part of the communications revolution will have easy access to the internet by 2005.

UK Online Centres will offer access and support in local communities, businesses and the high street to anyone who is interested in furthering their technology skills, including the internet. There are already 600 new centres nationwide, with a final total of 6000 by the end of 2002.

The Government's UK Online helpline will give you information on all the latest developments, including locations of your nearest public access point. It can also tell you about training courses running in your area. Call **0800 100 900** and start your internet journey!

Cybercafes are dotted all over the country – with helpful staff who can show you the basics of using the internet. It's a good way to start surfing without the commitment and expense of buying a computer. Many cybercafes also offer food and drinks, and are a fun place to spend a few hours as you begin your internet adventures. Look at the following directory to find a cybercafe in your area.

Name	Address & Telephone	Website	Spaces	Rates	Food/Drink?	Opening Hours
London						
Snack & Surf	78 Cromer St, London WC1H 8ER	**info@snack&surf.com**	15	£1/hour	Yes	Mon-Sat 09.00-21.00
Cybergate	3 Leigh Street, London WC1 9EW **020 7387 3810**	**cybergate.uk.com**	25	£2/hour	No	9.00-23.00 7 days
Cyberia Ealing	73 New Broadway Ealing, London W5 5AL **020 8840 3131**	**ealing.cyberiacafe.net**	25	£4/hour	Yes	11.00-22.00 7 days
Rainbow Cyber Centre	5 Kingsplace, Chiswick High Road, London W4 4HT **020 8994 0053**	**rainbowcyber.co.uk/.com**	8	£2/hour	Full café	Mon-Sat 11.00-19.00
A1 Internet Café	19 Leinster Terrace, London W2 3ET **020 7402 1177**	**a1ic.co.uk**	14	£4/hour	Hot/cold drinks	24 hours

Name	Address & Telephone	Website	Spaces	Rates	Food/Drink?	Opening Hours
London						
Internet Exchange	47-49 Queensway, London W2 **020 7792 5790**	**internet-exchange.co.uk**	15	£3.50/hour	Starbucks	Mon-Fri 07.30-22.30 Sat 08.30-22.30 Sun 09.30-22.30
Internet Exchange	Trocadero Centre, Coventry Street, London W1V **020 7437 3704**	**internet-exchange.co.uk**		£3.50/hour	Starbucks	Sun-Thurs 10.00-00.00 Fri-Sat 10.00-01.00
Playing Fields	143 Whitfield Street, London W1T 5EP **020 7383 5850**		20	£3/hour	Licensed bar	12.00-19.00 7 days
Internet User Group	114 Cleveland St, London W1P 5DN **020 7916 3466**	**helpfirst.co.uk**	8	£3/hour	No	10.30-20.30 7 days
Interc@fe	25 Great Portland Street, London W1N 5DB **020 7631 0063**	**intercafe.co.uk**	9	£5/hour	Yes	Mon-Fri 7.30-19.00 Sat 09.30-17.00

Name	Address & Telephone	Website	Spaces	Rates	Food/Drink?	Opening Hours
London						
Internet Exchange	125-127 Baker Street, London W1M 1SG **020 7224 5402**	**internet-exchange.co.uk**	36	£3.50/hour	Starbucks	Mon-Fri 08.00-22.00 Sat-Sun 10.00-22.00
Webshack	15 Devon St, London W1D 3RT **0207 4398000**	**webshack-café.com**	34	£2/hour	Licensed bar/ snacks	10.00-23.00 7 days
Databox Café Dotcom	4 Red Lion Street, Richmond, Middlesex TW9 1RW **020 8940 9540**	**databoxcafe.com**	30	£3/hour	Yes	09.00-20.00 7 days
Databox Café Dotcom	91 High Street, Teddington, Middlesex TW11 8HS **020 8940 9540**	**databoxcafe.com**	30	£3/hour	Yes	09.00-20.00 7 days
Fulham eBar	42-48 New Kings Rd Parsons Green, London SW6 4LF **020 7384 9746**	**ebar.co.uk**	18	£6/hour	Yes	Mon-Thurs 09.00-22.30 Fri 09.00-00.00 Sat 09.00-01.00 Sun 10.00-18.00

London

Name	Address & Telephone	Website	Spaces	Rates	Food/Drink?	Opening Hours
Internet Lounge	24A Earls Court Gardens SW5 0SZ **0207 3701734**		88	£1/hour	No	09.00-00.00 7 days
Brixton Internet Exchange	Brixton Library, Brixton, Oval, London SW2 1JQ **020 7926 1057**	iecafe.co.uk	23	£4/hour	No	Mon-Fri 10.00-19.45 Sat 09.00-15.45
Netstop/PC Workshop	87-89 Tooting High Street, Tooting, London SW17 0SU **020 8672 4844**	pcworkshop.co.uk	35	£3/hour	Vending machines only	Mon-Sat 09.00-23.00
Internet Journey	1421 London Rd, Norbury SW16 4AH	internet-journey.co.uk	15	£3/hour	No	11.00-22.00 7 days
Streetham Internet Exchage	Streatham Library, 63 Streatham High Road, London SW16 1PL	iecafe.co.uk		£1/hour	No	Mon-Sat 09.30-17.00

281

Name	Address & Telephone	Website	Spaces	Rates	Food/Drink?	Opening Hours
London						
Internet Exchange	117 Putney High St, Putney, London SW15 1SS **0208 7851485**	**internet-exchange.co.uk**	17	£3/hour	Coffee	Mon-Fri 07.30-01.30
C@fe.net	40 Sheen Lane, East Lane, London SW14 8LW **020 8255 4022**	**cafenet.uk.com**	6	£4/hour	Thai food	Mon-Thurs 11.00-21.00 Fri-Sat 11.00-19.00 Sun 11.00-17.00
Chelsea.com	391 Kings Rd, London SW10 0LR **020 7351 5511**	**chelsea-net.com**	30	£3.50/hour	Coffee and snacks	Mon-Thurs 08.00-22.00 Fri-Sat 08.00-19.00 Sun 10.00-18.00
Internet Café	22-24 Buckingham Palace Road, Victoria, London SW1 0QP **020 7233 5786**	**e-comstore.net**	20	£1.50/hour	Coffee and drinks	Mon-Fri 08.00-22.00 Sat 10.00-20.00 Sun 10.00-18.00
Easyeverything	9-13 Wilton Road, London SW1 **020 7482 9502**	**easyeverything.co.uk**	350	£1/hour	Coffee/tea	24 hours

Name	Address & Telephone	Website	Spaces	Rates	Food/Drink?	Opening Hours
London						
Surfdotcom Ltd	13 Deptford Church Street, London SE8 4RX	surf.netcafe.co.uk **020 8853 4272**	7	£2/hour	Snacks	Mon-Fri 11.00-21.00 Sat 11.00-17.30
Nellys.net	75 Trafalgar Road, Greenwich, London SE10 9TS **020 8853 4272**	nellys.net	5	£5/hour	Snacks and drinks	Mon-Sat 11.00-20.00 Sun 12.00-20.00
Imaging World Ltd	31 Station Lane, Hornchurch, London RM12 6SL **01708 479 063**	imagingworld.co.uk	20	£4/hour		Mon-Sat 09.00-20.00 Sat-Sun 09.00-00.00
Ecafe	40 Golders Green Road, London NW11 8LL **020 8922 7113**	ecafelondon.com	32	£2/hour	Coffee/tea	Mon-Fri 08.00-00.00
Interactive Traveller	12A High Road, Willesden Green, London NW10 2QG **020 8451 8975**		15	£1/hour	Yes	10.00-22.00 7 days

283

Name	Address & Telephone	Website	Spaces	Rates	Food/Drink?	Opening Hours
London						
Up Link Cyber Café	Unit 63-74 The Catacoombs, Stables Market, Camden NW1 8AH **020 7482 5282**	**uplinkcybercafe.co.uk**	12	£2.50/hour	Full menu	10.00-00.00 7 days
Internet Exchange	109-117 Marylebone Road, Marylebone Library, London NW1 5PS **020 7486 3161**		24	£4/hour	None	Mon-Fri 09.30-19.00 Sat 10.00-16.45
Cybergate	117 Euston Road, London NW1 25X **020 7383 2282**	**cybergate.uk.com**	12	£2/hour	No	09.00-23.00 7 days
Mocroplay	168 Ballards Lane, Finchley Central, London N3 1LP **020 8371 0422**	**eplay.co.uk**	8	£2.50/hour		10.00-21.00 7 days
Liberty Cyber Hall	Moon Lane, High Barnet EN5 5ST **020 8275 0234**		15	£1.50/hour	Coffee	09.00-21.00 7 days

Name	Address & Telephone	Website	Spaces	Rates	Food/Drink?	Opening Hours
London						
Web Solutions	Roman House, 9/10 College Terrace, London E3 5AN **0208 9811333**		10	£2/hour	No	Mon-Fri 09.00-20.00
Cyber Buffs	241 High Street, Walthamstow, London E17 **020 8520 8666**	**cyberbuffs.co.uk**				Mon-Sat 09.00-23.00 Sun 11.00-23.00
Internet Planet	338 Barking Rd, London E13 8HL	**internetplanet.co.uk**	15	£2/hour	No	Mon-Sat 10.00-22.00 Sun 10.00-20.00
Cyber Buffs	696 High Road, Leytonstone, London E11 **0208 539 9695**	**cyberbuffs.co.uk**				Mon-Sat 10.00-22.00 Sun 12.00-22.00

Name	Address & Telephone	Website	Spaces	Rates	Food/Drink?	Opening Hours
Home Counties and The South East						
Internet Point @ HC	109 Weston Rd, Brighton BN1 2AA **01273 772882**	**wh&c.co.uk**	26	£2.50/hour	Sweets and Cold drinks	Mon-Sat 09.00-21.00 Sun 11.00-21.00
Global Information Centre	22 Pevensey Road, Eastbourne, East Sussex BN21 5HP **01323 431 770**	**gic.co.uk**	12	£4.50/hour	Drinks	Mon-Sat 10.00-19.00 Sun 12.00-18.00
PC Corner	218 Portland Road, Hove, East Sussex BN3 5QT **01273 383848**	**pccorner.co.uk**	16	£2/hour	Drinks	Mon-Fri 10.00-20.00 Sat 12.00-18.00
Adur Research Centre Ltd	2 Tarmont Lane, Shoreham-by-Sea, West Sussex BN43 6DA **0127354 4441**	**adur.co.uk**	8	£3.50/hour	None	09.30-16.30 7 days
Web Junction	6 High St, Beckenham, Kent BR3 1AZ **0208 6630727**		10	£2/hour	Drinks	Mon-Fri 10.00-19.30 Sat 10.00-18.00 Sun 11.00-16.00

Name	Address & Telephone	Website	Spaces	Rates	Food/Drink?	Opening Hours
Home Counties and The South East						
Webs Net Café	2 Queen St, Colchester, Essex CO1 2PJ **01206 560400**	**pcemporium.co.uk**	15	£4/hour	Food and drink	Mon-Sat 10.00-18.30
Sipnsurf	68C Church Rd, Tiptree, Colchester, Essex CO5 0HB **01621 810700**	**sipnsurf.co.uk**	4	£4/hour	Yes	Mon-Sat 09.00-21.00 Wed 09.00-21.00
Cyberzone	1 Dingwall Road, Croydon, Surrey CR0 2NA **020 8681 6500**	**cyberzone.co.uk**	12	£3.50/hour	Snacks and drinks	Mon-Sat 09.30-21.30 Sun 11.00-20.00
The Hitching Post	164 London Road, Mitcham, Surrey CR4 3DL	**hitchingpost.co.uk**	10	£3/hour	Yes	Mon-Fri 09.00-20.00 Sun 11.00-18.00
Stacs Café	40 Queen St, Nuneaton CV11 5JX **0247 638845**	**smcpcs.co.uk**	6	£3/hour	Yes	Mon-Sat 11.00-18.00

Name	Address & Telephone	Website	Spaces	Rates	Food/Drink?	Opening Hours
Home Counties and The South East						
Cafenet	2-3 Phoenix Court, Guildford, Surrey **01483 451945**	**cafenet.uk.com**	9	£5/hour		Mon-Fri 10.00-18.00 Sat 09.00-17.00 Sun 11.00-17.00
Quarks Internet Café	7 Jeffries Passage, Guildford, Surrey GU1 4AP **01483 451166**		20	£6/hour	Yes	Mon-Sat 10.00-21.00 Sun 12.00-20.00
Internet Shop	9 The Parade, Trumps Green Road, Virginia Water, Surrey GU25 4EH **01344 845533**	**internetshop.co.uk**	10	£5/hour		Mon-Fri 10.00-18.00 Sat 10.30-15.30
Get Surfed	4-6 Peterborough Road, Harrow, Middlesex HA1 2BQ	**getsurf.co.uk**	10	£3/hour	Snacks and drinks	Mon-Sat 10.00-18.30
Bhi Net Centre	701 High Rd, Seven Kings, Essex IG3 8RH **020 8590 2500**	**bhi-netcentre.co.uk**	6	£2/hour		Mon-Sat 10.00-20.00 Sun 12.00-16.00

Name	Address & Telephone	Website	Spaces	Rates	Food/Drink?	Opening Hours
Home Counties and The South East						
Konai-Click Future	115A Burlington Road, New Maldon, Surrey KT3 4LR		26	£3/hour	Vending Machines only	09.00-23.00 7 days
Tolworth Digital Access and IT Learning Centre	37-39 The Broadway, Tolworth KT6 7DJ **020 8339 6950**	kingston.gov.uk	8	£2/hour	No	Mon-Fri 10.00-18.00 Sat 09.30-17.00
Eon	32 Rochester High Street, Rochester, Kent ME1 1LD	eoni.com	9	£3/hour	Snacks and drinks	10.00-20.00 7 days
Internet Exchange	8-12 George Street, Oxford OX1 2AF		42	£5/hour	No	08.00-20.00 7 days
Mices.com	118A Highstreet, Oxford OX1 4BX **01865 726364**	www.mices.com	22	£3/hour	Yes	08.00-20.00 7 days

Home Counties and The South East

Name	Address & Telephone	Website	Spaces	Rates	Food/Drink?	Opening Hours
Quarks	7 Union Street, Reading RG1 1EU **0118 9572937**	**www.quark.co.uk**	16	£5/hour	Yes	Mon-Sat 07.30-21.00 Sun 10.00-19.00
Nethouse	13 London Road, Barthing, Essex RG1 8AA **020 8591 4777**	**www.nethouseportal.com**	12	£1/hour	Drinks	24 hours
Newbury Internet	Unit 2, Kendrick House, Wharf Street, Newbury RG14 5AP **01635 569123**			£6/hour	No	24 hours
Sharatech Internet	69 Ilfield Rd, West Green, Crawley, West Sussex RH117BB **01293 419180**	**www.sharatech.com**	11	£3/hour	Yes	10.00-20.00 7 days
Xcession	52 Walsworth Rd, Hitchin, Herts SG4 9SX **01462 625549**		12	£5/hour	Snacks	Mon-Fri 10.00-10.00 Sat 10.00-18.00 Sun 12.00-18.00

Name	Address & Telephone	Website	Spaces	Rates	Food/Drink?	Opening Hours
Home Counties and The South East						
Reef	16 Bridge Street, Bishopstalkford, Herts SM23 2JY	reef.co.uk	4	£4/hour	Yes	Mon-Sat 10.00-21.00
Beaten Track	Chippenham Railway Station, Cocklebury Rd, Chippenham SN15 5EQ **01249 448002**	beatentrack.net			Food and drink	Mon-Thurs 05.30-22.00 Fri-Sat 08.30-23.00 Sun 08.30-20.30
South West						
Click Café	Mavar Street, Bath BA1		12	£4/hour	Snacks and drinks	Mon-Sun 10.00-10.00
Virtual Realm	4 Cle Terrace, Bath BA1 5DF **01225 447466**		17	£3/hour	Yes	10.00-22.00 7 days

Name	Address & Telephone	Website	Spaces	Rates	Food/Drink?	Opening Hours
South West						
Cyber Place	132 Charminster Road, Bournemouth BH8 8UU **0120 468 766**	**cyberplace.co.uk**	30	£2/hour	Yes	09.00–00.00 7 days
ARC Interacive	27 Broad Street, Bristol BS1					
Netgates	51 Broadgates, Bristol BS1 2EJ **0117 9074000**	**netgates.co.uk/café**	20	£5/hour	Yes	Mon–Fri 09.30–18.00 Sat 10.30–17.30
Internet Café	140 White Lady's Road, Clifton, Bristol BS8 2RS **0117 973 6323**	**internet-café.org.uk**	30	£2/hour	Yes	Mon–Fri 09.30–18.00
Hyperactive Internet Café	1B Central Station Crescent, Queen Street, Exeter EX4 3SB **01392 201544**	**hyperactive-café.co.uk**	8	£5/hour	Snacks and drinks	Mon–Fri 09.30–18.00 Sat 10.30–17.30

Name	Address & Telephone	Website	Spaces	Rates	Food/Drink?	Opening Hours
South West						
Cyberfish	44 Long Street, Wotton-under-Edge, Gloucester GL12 7BT **01453 844108**		6	£3.50/hour	Snacks and drinks	Mon-Sat 09.00-22.00
Loft	8-9 Henrietta Street, Cheltenham GL50 4AA **01242 539 573**		9	£3/hour	Snacks and drinks	Mon-Sat 10.00-18.00
Tucan Internet	Cheltenham House, The Square, Stow on the Wold GL54 1AB **01451 870609**	**tucaninternet.co.uk**	5	£5.50/hour	Snacks	Mon-Sat 10.00-18.00
Internet Exchange	The Bargate Centre, Southampton OI4 2YD **02380 233548**		30	£3/hour	No	Mon-Sat 09.00-21.00 Sun 10.00-18.00
Carp Computers	32 Frankfort Gate, Plymouth PL1 1QD **01752 221777**	**city-computers.net**	9	£5/hour	Free coffee/tea	Mon-Sat 09.00-18.00

Name	Address & Telephone	Website	Spaces	Rates	Food/Drink?	Opening Hours
South West						
Internet Junction	2 Southgate, Chichester PO19 2DJ **01243 776644**	**internet-junction.com**	12	£2.50/hour	Snacks	Mon-Fri 10.00-21.00 Sat 10.00-16.00
Ecafe	15A High Street, Bognor Regis, W.Sussex PO21 4JP	**ecafe.co.uk**	12	£4.50/hour	Snacks and drinks	Mon-Sat 10.00-18.00
Cyber Café	1C Albert Rd, Portsmouth PO5 2SE **029 286 4158**	**cyber/southsea.co.uk**	10	£2/hour	Drinks	Mon-Sat 10.30-21.00 Sun 12.00-18.00
Interstep	84A Middle St, Yeovil, Somerset BA20 1LT **01935 420317**	**interstep.demon.co.uk**	7	£4.50/hour	Yes	Tues-Sat 10.00-16.00
Hyperion	67 High Street, Swanage, BH19 2LY Dorset **01929 475614**	**hyperion-café.co.uk**	5	£4/hour	Snacks and drinks	Mon-Fri 09.00-17.00

Name	Address & Telephone	Website	Spaces	Rates	Food/Drink?	Opening Hours
South West						
Access All Areas	Grosvenor Hs, 19 Western Rd, Weymouth, Dorset DT4 8NU **01305 781001**	**weymouth-info.co.uk**	12	£5/hour	Tea /Coffee	Mon-Sun 10.00-22.00
Project Cosmic	The Station, Exeter Road, Otterley St Mary, Devon EX11 1AH **01404 813226**	**cosmic.org.uk**	8	£3.50/hour	Drinks	Mon-Fri 09.00-17.00 Fri-Sat 09.00-21.00
Kianna Café	4 The Mall, Bridge Street, Andover SP10 1QL **01264 363690**		30	£2/hour	Yes	Mon-Sat 09.00-17.00
The Numinous Café	29 East St, Asburton, South Devon TQ13 7AQ **01364 652508**	**numinouscafe.co.uk**	5	£4/hour	Food and Drink	Tues-Sat 12.00-21.00
Net-zone	6 Newton Road, Torquay TQ2 5BW **01803 291215**	**net-zone.co.uk**	6	£2.80/hour	Drinks	Mon-Sat 09.30-18.00

Name	Address & Telephone	Website	Spaces	Rates	Food/Drink?	Opening Hours
South West						
Puffin Technology Ltd	Crown House, 48 Totnes Road, Paignton, Devon TQ4 5JY **01803 698257**	**puffincomputers.co.uk**	12	£5/hour	Yes	09.00-21.00 7 days
Cybersurf @Newquay	2 Broad Street, Newquay **01637 875 497**		6	£1/hour	coffee/Tea	10.00-22.00 7 days
Cyberlink Café	2A Barnack Road, Blandford Forum, Dorset **01258 459157**		2	£5/hour	Yes	Mon-Sat 09.00-17.00
I-Café	30 Milford St, Salisbury, Wiltshire SB5 2AP **01722 320050**	**ifunk.co.uk**	8	£4/hour	Snacks and drinks	Mon 10.00-21.00 Tues-Fri 11.00-21.00 Sat 10.00-21.00
Salisbury Cyber Café	62 Winchester St, Salisbury, Wiltshire SP1 1HL		10	£5/hour	Tea/coffee	Mon-Sat 12.00-00.00

Name	Address & Telephone	Website	Spaces	Rates	Food/Drink?	Opening Hours
Central England						
Internet Exchange	The Pallisade Shopping Centre, Birmingham B2 4JX **0121 633 9803**		18	£4/hour	No	Mon-Sat 07.00-23.00 Sun 10.00-23.00
Orange Studio	Cannon Street, Birmingham B2 5EP **0800 079 0909**	**orangestudio.co.uk**	24	£4/hour	Snacks and drinks	Mon-Sat 08.30-18.00
The Surfshack	287 Birchfield Rd, Perrybarr, Birmingham B20 3DD **0121 2500113**		12	£3/hour	Drinks	Mon-Sat 12.00-18.00
Net Adventure Cyber Café	68-70 Dalton Street, Birmingham B4 7LX **0121 693 6655**	**netadventure.co.uk**	25	£3/hour	Yes	10.00-22.00 7 days
Log on Log off	467 Barewood Road, Birmingham B66 4DH **0121 420 4343**		3	£5/hour	Yes	Mon-Fri 10.00-18.00 Sat 09.00-18.00

Name	Address & Telephone	Website	Spaces	Rates	Food/Drink?	Opening Hours
Central England						
Web Internet café	60–66 Litchfield Rd, Sutton Cold, W. Midlands B74 2NA **0121 321 3528**		30	£5/hour	Snacks and drinks	08.00–22.00 7 days
Sutton Court Hotel	66 Lichfield Rd, Sutton Coldfield, Birmingham, West Midlands B74 2NA **0121 3213528**	scit.co.uk	30	£3/hour	Snacks	Mon–Sun 08.00–22.00
Bon Java	Derridge Train Station, Solihull, West Midlands B93 85A **01564 774 474**			£5/hour	Yes	Mon–Fri 06.30–17.00
Sitnsurf	5 Cocoa Yard, Nantwitch, Cheshire CW5 5BL **01270 625582**	sitnsurf.co.uk	7	£4/hour	Drinks	Mon–Sat 10.30–17.30
Coffee Culture	3 New Street, Burton-on-Street, Staffordshire DE14 3QN **01283 569922**	coffee-culture.co.uk	5	£4/hour	Snacks and drinks	Mon–Sat 09.00–19.30

Name	Address & Telephone	Website	Spaces	Rates	Food/Drink?	Opening Hours
Central England						
Spiders Web	Cleveland St, Doncaster DN1 2VZ **01302 814777**	**webspiders.co.uk**	5	£2.50/hour	Yes	10.00-23.00 7 days
The Arena	144 High St, Stourbridge, West Midlands DY8 1DW **01384 377165**	**arena-cybercafe.co.uk**	20	£4/hour	Yes	Mon-Thurs 9.30-21.00 Fri 09.30-19.00
Dot.com	Parson Lane, Clitheroe, Lancashire **01200 427700**	**eclitheroe.co.uk**	6	£2/hour	Snacks and drinks	Mon-Fri 11.00-18.00 Sat 11.00-16.30
Tea Too Internet Café	Lake Road, Windermere, Cumbria LA23 2JJ **01539 445657**		4	£4/hour	Snacks and drinks	7 days
The Green Room	62 Euston Rd, Morecombe, Lancashire LA4 5DG **01524 425481**	**green-room.co.uk**	1	£6/hour	Yes	Mon-Sat 10.00-16.00

Name	Address & Telephone	Website	Spaces	Rates	Food/Drink?	Opening Hours
Central England						
Netspace	78 Baxtergate, Laighborough, Leicestershire LE11 1TT **01509 269999**	**net-space.co.uk**	14	£2.25/hour	Yes	Mon-Fri 09.00-21.00 Sat 10.00-16.00
Stayfree Internet Café	Lilly House, 1A Cardif St, Leicester LE2 0JN **0116 2230303**	**stayfree.co.uk**	8	£4/hour	Snacks	Mon-Sat 11.00-19.00
Source	Unit 3, Macadam House, Cadzow Lane, Hamilton ML3 6AY **01698 207227**		12	£4/hour	Snacks and drinks	09.00-19.00 7 days
The IT Café	Park Road Resource Centre, 53 Park Road, Woodham, Nottingham NG19 8ER **01623 414038**	**it-cybercafe.co.uk**	9	£4/hour	Snacks	Mon-Fri 11.00-19.00
Rush	5 St Maris St, Stanford, Lincolnshire PE9 2DE **01780 767874**	**rush.uk.com**	15	£3/hour	Yes	Mon-Sat 09.00-20.00 Sun 10.00-18.00

Name	Address & Telephone	Website	Spaces	Rates	Food/Drink?	Opening Hours
Central England						
Java's Internet Coffee House	8 Stephen's Place, Chesterfield S41 1XL **01246 274455**		40	£3/hour	Yes	Mon-Fri 08.00-18.00
Kavehaz	103 Mill Street, Macclesfield, Cheshire SK11 6NN **01625 262611**		3	£4/hour	Yes	Mon-Sat 08.00-10.00
Peak Art	30 Market Street, Highpeak, Derbyshire SK22 4AE **01663 747770**		25	£6/hour	Yes	09.30-17.30 7 days
The North						
Saints	Back Silver St, Durham DH1 1SQ	**saints.durham.co.uk**	2	£3/hour	Yes	10.00-18.00 7 days

Name	Address & Telephone	Website	Spaces	Rates	Food/Drink?	Opening Hours
The North						
Interworld	2/6 Commercial Street, Halifax HX1 17A **01422 356097**	**halifaxinternet.com**	4	£3/hour	Yes	Mon-Sat 10.00-17.00
Megabyte Cybercafe	14 Hyde ParkCorner, Leeds LS6 1AS **0113 275 4715**	**megabytecybercafe.co.uk**	10	£2.50/hour		Mon-Sat 10.00-16.00
Mouse House	3 Wellfield Place, Headingley, Leeds LS6 3HA **0113 274 2533**		6	£4/hour	Drinks	Mon-Fri 11.00-18.30 Sat-Sun 11.00-18.00
Yes Cyber	131 Chapel Town Leeds LS7 3DU **0113 262 0794**		7	£2/hour	Tea/coffee	Mon-Fri, 10.00-18.00 Sat 11.00-16.00
Cyberia Manchester	12 Oxford Street, Manchester M1 5AN **0161 950 2233**	**cyberiacafe.net**	30	£2/hour	Yes	Mon-Fri 09.00-23.00 Sat 11.00-23.00

Name	Address & Telephone	Website	Spaces	Rates	Food/Drink?	Opening Hours
The North						
Café Disc	223-225 High Street,	**capedisc.com**	8	4/hour, 3/half hour, women only internet access	Yes	Mon-Thurs 09.00-18.00 Fri 09.00-17.00
E2E Internet	130 St Albans Road, Watford WD2 4AE	**escape2e.net**	16	£3.50/hours	Snacks and drinks	Mon-Fri 12.00-21.00 Sat 12.00-18.00
DIY Internet Point	1 Park Road, Batley, W. Yorks WF17 5LP **01924 479908**		7	£3/hours	Yes	Mon-Fri 10.30-20.00 Sat-Sun 12.00-18.00
Gateway Internet café/Bar	26 Swinegate, York, Yorkshire YO1 8AZ **01904 646 446**	**ymn.net/gateway**	6	£4/hour	Snacks and drinks (free access from 8pm)	Mon-Wed 10.00-23.00
Easyeverything	8 Exchange Street, Manchester **020 7907 7800**	**easyeverything.co.uk**	375	From £1/hour	Coffee/tea	24 hours

Name	Address & Telephone	Website	Spaces	Rates	Food/Drink?	Opening Hours
The North						
Mcnulty's Internet Exchange	26-30 Market Street, Newcastle **0191 230 1280**	**internet-change.co.uk**	30	£3/hour	Yes	Mon-Sat 09.00-20.00 Sun 12.00-16.00
East Anglia						
UK Cybercafe	Saxhall Place, 46 Magdalane St, Norwich NR3 1JU **01603 612643**	**ukcybercafe.co.uk**	5	£6/hour	Tea/Coffee	Mon-Fri 10.00-19.30 Sat 10.00-17.00 Sun 10.00-16.00
RJT Internet Services	Great Yarmouth, Norfolk NR30 1PU **01493 857048**	**rjt.co.uk**	4	£3/hour	Drinks	Tue-Sat 09.00-17.00
The BECS Internet Stop	74-75 Victoria Road, Great Yarmouth, Norfolk NR30 3BA **01493 330 498**	**becs.fsbusiness.co.uk**	4	£3/hour	Drinks	Mon-Fri 09.30-20.00 Sat & Sun 09.30-17.00

Name	Address & Telephone	Website	Spaces	Rates	Food/Drink?	Opening Hours
East Anglia						
Peterborough Cyber Café	Keeble Chambers, Calgate, Peterborough PE1 1DA **01733 421808**		16	£2.50/hour	Drinks	Mon–Fri 09.00–20.00 Sat 10.00–18.00
Loafers	1–3 Alexander Road, Wisbech, Cambridge PE13 1HQ **01945 583861**		2	£6/hour	Yes	Mon–Sat 09.00–15.00
International Telecomms Centre	2 Wheeler Street, Cambridge CB2 3QB **01223 357 358**		12	£3.50/hour		09.00–00.00 7 days
Wales						
Over the Top	36 Kirkgate, Cockermouth, Cumbria CA13 9PJ **01900 827016**	**overthetopcafe.co.uk**	44	£6/hour	Yes	Wed–Sat 10.30–16.00

Name	Address & Telephone	Website	Spaces	Rates	Food/Drink?	Opening Hours
Wales						
Cardiff Cybercafe	9 Duke Street, 1st Floor, Cardiff CF10 1AY	**cardiffcybercafe.co.uk**	10	£4.50/hour	No	Mon-Fri 10.00-19.00 Sat 10.00-18.00 Sun 11.00-17.00
Cardiff Internet Café	17 Wyndham Arcade, Cardiff CF10 1FH **02920 232313**	**relaxinternetcafe.com**	27	£3/hour	Snacks and drinks	Mon-Sat 09.30-21.00 Sat 10.00-19.00
123 Computers	11 Watergate, Brecon LD3 9AN **0187 611 929**	**2x3.net**	6	£2/hour		Mon-Sat 09.00-17.00
Dimension 4	4 Bangor Street, Canaervon LL55 1AT **01286 678 777**	**dimension4.co.uk**	3	£2/hour	Yes	Mon-Sat 10.00-18.00
Ystalyfera Development Trust	The Railway, 72 Commercial St, Ystalyfera, Neath, Port Talbot SA9 2HS **01639 843965**		20	£2.50/hour	Snacks and drinks	Mon-Fri 09.00-17.00 Wed 07.00-21.00

Name	Address & Telephone	Website	Spaces	Rates	Food/Drink?	Opening Hours
Scotland						
Web 13	13 Bread St, Edinburgh EH 9AL **0131 2298883**	**webb.co.uk**	18	£3/hour	Snacks and drinks	
International 52 Telecomms Centre	High Street, The Royal Mile, Edinburgh EH1 1TB **0131 558 7114**		24	£1/hour		09.00-23.00 7 days
Tinsley Lockhart	66-68 Thistle St, Edinburgh EH2 1EN **0131 225 5000**		5	£3.50/hour and drinks	Snacks	Mon-Fri 09.00-22.00
First Net Online	1A Broughan Place, Edinburgh EH3 9HW	**frugal-café.com**	50	£1/hour	Snacks and drinks	08.30-22.00 7 days
Inform/Due South Ltd	44 West Oreston St, Edinburgh EH8 9PY **0131 466 7767**	**T2LG.net.org**	15	£3/hours	Yes	Mon-Sat 08.00-20.00

Name	Address & Telephone	Website	Spaces	Rates	Food/Drink?	Opening Hours
Scotland						
Gig@bytes	5 St Paul's Square, Perth PH1 5QW **01738 451580**	**gig-at-bytes.com**	8	£5/hour,	Coffee/tea	Mon-Sat 10.00-18.30 Sun 12.00-17.00
Easyeverything	58 Rose Street, Edinburgh **020 7907 7800**	**easyeverything.co.uk**	450	From £1/hour	Coffee/tea	24 hours
Easyeverything	57-61 Vincent Street, Glasgow **020 7907 7800**	**easyeverything.co.uk**	375	From £1 hour	Coffee/tea	24 hours

Name	Address & Telephone	Website	Spaces	Rates	Food/Drink?	Opening Hours
Northern Ireland						
Paradigm Internet Café	16 West Street, Caricksergus BT38 7AR **0289 336 1531**			£5/hour	Yes	Mon-Sat 10.00-16.00
Barnam	303 Upper Newtownards, Belfast BT4 35H **0289 065 6807**		3	£4/hour		Mon-Sat 10.00-21.00
Bean-there.com	20 The Diamond, Derry BT48 6HP **02871 281 303**	**bean-there.com**	6	£4.50/hour	Coffees and snacks	Mon-Sat 09.00-19.00 Sun 14.00-18.00
Globe Café	43 Kingsgate Street, Coleraine, N. Ireland BT52 1LD **02870 326619**	**theglobalcafe.co.uk**	12	£4/hour	Snacks and drinks	Mon-Sat 10.00-18.00
Cyber Perk	11d Managham Street, Newry, County Down BT35 6BB **028302 52303**	**cyberperkcafe.net**	8	£4.50/hour	Yes	Mon-Sat 09.30-20.00

Name	Address & Telephone	Website	Spaces	Rates	Food/Drink?	Opening Hours
The Islands						
Feesans Lounge	22 Duke Street, Douglas, Isle of Man IM1 2AY **01624 679280**	**feesan.co.uk**	12	£4/hour	Snacks and drinks	Mon-Sat 09.00-19.00
Use The Internet	6 Sand St, St Helier, Jersey, Channel Islands JE2 3QP **01534 731121**	**easyinternet.co.uk**	11	£4/hour	Snacks	Mon-Fri 10.00-20.00 Sat 10.00-17.30
The Harbour Café	16 East Princes St, Rothesay, Isle of Bute PA20 **01700 505166**	**isle-of-bute.com**	1	£45/hour	Yes	Mon-Sun 10.00-18.00 except Tues